THE DECORATOR'S GUIDE
TO FABRICS, WALLPAPERS, RUGS AND TRIMMINGS

JENNIE ELIAS & JANE MORRIS OF PERCY BASS

Malabar, Jaipur Collection

THE DECORATOR'S GUIDE
TO FABRICS, WALLPAPERS, RUGS AND TRIMMINGS

JENNIE ELIAS & JANE MORRIS OF PERCY BASS

Produced by SPG Media Limited

SPG MEDIA LIMITED

Art Director Henrik Williams

Project Manager Roberta Ricciotti

Layout by Roberto Filistad & Joanna Bettles

Edited by James Hope & Daniel Watson

Published by

Percy Bass Limited

Cover image: Brunschwig & Fils,
photograph Anthony Cotsifas
Back cover image: Jim Thompson

Copyright © 2006 Percy Bass Limited. All rights reserved. No part of this publication may be reproduced, stored in a retrieval system or transmitted in any form or by any means, electronic, photocopying or otherwise, without prior permission of the publisher and copyright owner. Whilst every effort has been made to ensure the accuracy of the information in this publication, the publisher accepts no responsibility for errors or omissions.

Printed in China

ISBN: 0 9552007 0 9
ISBN: 978 0 9552007 0 0

Romo, Nara Stripe Charcoal wallpaper

Contents

Northcroft Fabrics, Limoges and Loire in brick red cotton/modacrylic damask

Alton-Brooke, Needlepoint rug

11	Allsignsgroup	57	Evertrading Ltd.
12	Alton-Brooke	58	Eclipse Carpets
16	Anta	60	J. Brooke Fairbairn & Company
17	ARC Collections Limited	61	Fetherstonhaugh Fabrics
18	Ariadne	62	Fired Earth
20	Atmosphere	64	Fitzroy Fabrics
22	G P & J Baker	65	Anna French
24	Beaudesert	66	Fox Linton
26	Beaumont & Fletcher	68	The Gainsborough Silk Weaving Company
27	Bennett Silks	70	Garin 1820
28	Luigi Bevilacqua	71	Hamilton Weston
30	Sabina Fay Braxton	72	James Hare Silks
32	Borderline	74	Nicholas Herbert Ltd.
35	Busby & Busby	75	Heritage Trimmings
36	John Boyd Textiles	76	Allegra Hicks
38	Brunschwig & Fils	77	Hodsoll McKenzie
40	Cabbages & Roses	78	Holland & Sherry
41	Chase Erwin	80	Humphries Weaving Company
42	Chelsea Textiles	82	Interdesign UK
43	Coromandel Crafts Ltd.	83	Kathryn Ireland
44	Cole & Son	84	The Isle Mill
46	Colefax and Fowler	86	Jab International Furnishings Ltd.
48	de Gournay	88	Kenzo Maison
50	Designers Guild	89	Robert Kime
52	Donatus	90	Krams Ugo
54	Jason D'Souza		
56	Jim Dickens		

The Percy Bass Decorator's Guide

B, Villaverde

Brian Yates, New Botanicals Butterfly Ball

William Potts, Louis XV Commode by Moissonnier

91	Brian Lawrence	135	Deborah Rolt Rugs
92	Lee Jofa	136	Sandberg
94	Lelievre	137	The Silk Gallery
96	Lewis & Wood	138	Ian Sanderson
100	Linwood	140	Smith & Brighty
102	The Malabar Cotton Company	142	George Spencer Designs
103	Marvic Textiles	146	Stuart Interiors
104	Natasha Marshall	148	Tassinari & Chatel
106	Marimekko	150	Dr Brian J. Taylor & Son
107	Christopher Moore	152	Titchfield
108	Mulberry Home	154	Titley & Marr
110	Jean Monro Ltd.	156	Jim Thompson
112	Henry Newbery & Co Ltd.	158	Bernard Thorp & Co Ltd.
114	Northcroft Fabrics	160	Today Interiors
115	nya nordiska	161	Trimmings By Design
116	Nouveau Fabrics	162	Turnell & Gigon Distribution
118	Nursery Window	164	Vervain
120	Roger Oates	166	Voyage Decoration
122	Les Olivades	168	Warner Fabrics
123	Orchard Fabrics	170	Warwick Fabrics
124	Emma P Fabrics	172	Watts of Westminster
126	Tim Page Carpets	174	Johannes Wellman Fabrics
128	Parkertex	176	Whitchurch Silk Mill
130	William Potts Limited	177	Fran White
131	Pongees Silks	178	Brian Yates
132	PWC International Ltd.	180	Zimmer + Rohde
134	Reymondon Trimmings	182	Zoffany

Beaudesert, 'Polo' linen in ochre colourway

Percy Bass Limited

184 Walton St, London SW3 2JL
Tel +44 (0)20 7589 4853 Fax: +44 (0)20 7581 4137 E-mail: PercyBass@aol.com Web: www.PercyBass.com

Foreword

Never a day goes by without someone telephoning and asking me which company supplies a particular fabric or wallpaper. We decided to publish this book to try to provide a comprehensive guide to fabric and wallpaper suppliers and their products.

I have run Percy Bass for 25 years and I feel there has never been such an amazing choice of fabrics and wallpapers as there is now. Having come through a rather bland phase in interior decoration, influenced by minimalism, it is wonderful to see colour back in fashion.

A lot of the companies in the book are 'trade-only', but Percy Bass would be delighted to supply anything described in the book and send samples as requested.

I do hope you enjoy the book and do keep ringing me if you need any help!

Jane Morris

Mulberry Home, Romantic Heros collection

8

The Percy Bass Decorator's Guide

Watts of Westminster, Peaseblossom

Above: JAB, Orlando
Below: Bennett Silks, Como devoré
Bottom: Noveau Fabrics, Melbourne

Introduction

There is now, more than ever, a vast array of choice in interior design. Magazines and television programmes have stimulated interest in the art form of interior decoration to such an extent that most customers now have their own opinions about their ideal room and favourite colour scheme. Visual stimulation from travelling to different parts of the world has also been hugely inspirational to the world of decorating. This has manifested itself not just in Mediterranean and European styles, but has been influenced by Asian and even African artistic traditions.

Although interior style does not change as frequently or as dramatically as the world of fashion, moods do change through gradual evolution. At times the trend can appear cyclical, as the contemporary recurrence of Art Deco and of 1970s motifs has shown. However, it is never a pastiche; the designs coming out of design libraries have been freshened with contemporary tastes and are blended differently to give a new interpretation, creating something truly avant-garde.

Traditional designs have never appeared dated, but the current inclination is to pair down from the frilly, cluttered look of the mid 1980s, with floral motifs being predominately printed on linen instead of the traditional cotton chintz, and in muted colour combinations. Today's classics flow with a more neutral palette, although trimmings, unappealing to minimalists, are now resurfacing on cushions and curtains.

Wallpapers have become ever bolder in scale and colouration. They can add a dramatic effect to a room, often used on one wall only. Colours too are bold, sometimes featuring silver and gold figurations on purple, lime green, turquoise or monochrome black and white.

Today's rugs, increasingly designed to complement wood flooring, can be custom-made to match any interior, either in strong contemporary tones or more traditional designs such as Zeiglers. They make a prominent impact on design and can help to unify the hues and textures of the various fabrics used in a particular room.

Every colour in the rainbow is represented in the fabrics, wallpapers, trimmings and rugs in this book. Colour, of course, depends on personal taste, but should also be relevant to the style of furnishings used

The Percy Bass Decorator's Guide

Right: Reymondon Trimmings, Osier tiebacks
Above: nya nordiska, Gira & Girlanda
Below: Warwick Fabrics, Mayfair collection

in a room. The ever popular creams, beiges and soft whites can form a neutral backdrop to a contemporary or traditional room and create an atmosphere of calm and harmony. Colour can be added in textiles to add contrast and help to define space and the mood of a room. The decorator's palette changes with his or her perception of fashion. Taupe and soft grey/greens and aqua are currently popular, as are lilac and purple. The combinations are fresh too – olive greens with aubergine, chocolate with aqua. The use of browns and oranges as complementary colours, in the manner of David Hick's designs of the 1960s, is also making a comeback.

The traditional country colours of dark greens and reds are timeless and can easily be updated for a more vibrant effect by adding, for instance, Mogul-inspired cushions or trimmings made of leather or crystal beads.

Together these various stimuli have culminated in an explosion of choice for the decorator and the customer. There is never only one style of the moment and this book has aimed to present this endless variety and to explain the stories and specialities behind the pattern books. The decorative style of a particular textile company, for example, can no longer be pigeon-holed as specialising in only the traditional or only the contemporary. The established companies usually offer a mixture of several choices of style and collections. Several also produce their own wallpapers and trimmings. This guide is to help define each company and show examples of what they offer to the market.

An interior designer should be an expert at drawing different elements together to create something original and unique, tailored to meet the specific tastes of a discerning client. They should understand the importance of lighting, comfort, scale and colour. This guide is aimed at assisting the work of the decorator and hopefully exposes the decorator to fresh design inspirations, allowing them to broaden their stylistic base.

The Percy Bass Decorator's Guide

Allsignsgroup

A large format printer and signage specialist based in West London, Allsignsgroup has been trading for over 45 years and is one of London's most technologically advanced and progressive signage companies.

Top left: Sample of barrel fixing with a print reverse-mounted to Perspex sheet; Above, from top: Marketing suite for prestigious property development in West London; Wallpaper project at Krisy Kreme head offices in West London; Allsignsgroup facilities in West London, showing a Scitex large format solvent inkjet printer

The latest technology in large format printing has now reached the interior market with quite a splash. Recent advances in ink and media technology allow Allsignsgroup to output single or multiple prints onto material suitable for interior design markets. The company print with UV-stable water- or solvent-based inks, depending on requirements, at resolutions up to 1200dpi. The result is an incredibly vibrant high resolution print, ideal for both interior and exterior applications.

The most exciting development is a fabric-based wall covering, which is class 0 and 1 fire rated. It allows printing directly to its surface. Supplied at 1500mm wide, it allows application of paste directly to the wall, leading to easy installation, seamless joins and fantastic print quality. Other media for the interior market include standard wallpaper, blue-backed temporary papers, photographic gloss and satins, artist grade watercolour papers, clear film and mesh for building wraps.

UV inkjet technology also allows print to canvas and cottons. Expert in-house framing service complements this ability perfectly. Stretching the canvas onto artist grade wooden stretcher bars. These come in a variety of sizes allowing canvas prints up to 1.4m x 3m. Grand format printers will allow for prints from 2.8m wide to 6m wide.

In-house designers can produce finished artwork to help you achieve your look whether it is a private residence, office, bar or restaurant. Complementing the printing and design services is an extensive property, retail and architectural signage service, and a nationwide fitting service.

Allsignsgroup is a member of Investors in People and Future Forest's Carbon Neutral programme.

Contact Details

Allsignsgroup
Crown House
30 Commerce Road
Brentford
Middlesex
TW8 8LE
Tel: 08707 577755
Fax: 020 8232 6801
ISDN: 020 8847 1966
Email: sales@allsignsgroup.com
Website: www.allsignsgroup.com

The Percy Bass Decorator's Guide

Needlepoint NP-067

Rugs are a passion at Alton-Brooke, where they have spent three decades building close relationships with weavers from around the world to complement the company's extensive fabric collections.

From India Alton-Brooke offers dhurries woven in wool and cotton. Woven since the first century as floor coverings, the dhurrie was traditionally used in palaces as an under carpet for hand-knotted carpets, which could be easily rolled away to leave a bright, cool dhurrie for the summer.

From India and China there are fine soumaks, boasting authentic designs inspired by years of research into ancient Persian design and historic carpets from around the world. These are classically woven using a mixture of vegetable and chrome dyes to give an authentic antique finish.

Carpets from India, China and Pakistan include hand-knotted chobi, ziegler, savonnerie and other traditional designs. From Europe there are a large number of contemporary manufactured carpets in wool, linen, jute, sisal and seagrass, all available with leather, suede and fabric borders made to order. And from Turkey, Monrovia and Andalusia there are kelims in a multitude of colours and designs.

Alton-Brooke offers a bespoke rug-making service to the client's specifications. Recent projects include hand-knotted rugs for the British ambassador's residence in Madrid.

Contact Details

Alton-Brooke
2–25 Chelsea Harbour Design Centre
Lots Road
London
SW10 0XE
Tel: 020 7376 7008
Fax: 020 7376 7009
Email: info@alton-brooke.co.uk
Website: www.alton-brooke.co.uk

With an extensive range of fabrics to draw on, Alton-Brooke can offer bespoke rugs and carpets from all over the world, from India to Andalusia.

Alton-Brooke

Millennia MI-19 Rust

Millennia MI-25 Gold

The Percy Bass Decorator's Guide

Above: Rug showing the colours of the Keystone Collection;
Right: Azam Cream Navy Cotton Dhurrie; Inset, from top:
Turkana 17 Khaki Kombi black leather suede 35 Ceniza;
Bereber 02 Duna Bound Zebra; Bereber 02 Duna Bound Ginetta

The Percy Bass Decorator's Guide

Above: Leather Bound Pulp 03 Bound Pequino Crocodile Verde with Antelope Fur Rug; Inset from top: Bereber 02 Duna Bound Ostrich Marron; Bereber 02 Duna Bound Nutria; Bereber 02 Duna Bound Puma

The Percy Bass Decorator's Guide

Clockwise, from left: Dining room, six dining chairs upholstered in Donina Stewart 100 per cent worsted wool, large Ballone carpet rug 100 per cent wool; Wallcovering, 50m Highland Club tartan 100 per cent worsted wool, three dining chairs upholstered in Duncan glen 100 per cent worsted wool; Cushions (back to front) Loch Lochy and Neil Gunn 100 per cent wool 55 x 55cm, Paint ancient blue eggshell

Contact Details

Anta
55 Sloane Square
London
SW1W 8AX
Tel: 020 7730 4773

Crocket's Land
91–93 West Bow
Victoria Street
Edinburgh
EH1 2JP
Tel: 0131 225 4616
Website: www.anta.co.uk

Anta

Founded by husband and wife Lachlan and Annie Stewart, an architect and a textile designer respectively, Anta is a Scottish home furnishings and accessories company based in Fearn, in the north-east Highlands.

Making pottery and woven textiles in the north of Scotland, Anta collections use soft, muted colours inspired by the natural beauty of the Scottish landscape. The company uses only the best materials and traditional skills to create unique pieces for the home.

Fabrics and furniture
The company's natural fabrics range from classic woollen tartans and tweeds to more contemporary textured plains and herringbones. Designs for new wool weaves are reworked from traditional tartans, resulting in stunning colour combinations. Oak-legged stools are also available, covered in these natural fabrics. Anta also makes bespoke solid oak furniture.

Accessories
Accessorising is the easiest way to add interest to or change the look and feel of a room. Anta's new collection of soft lambswool throws are coloured in muted landscape colours. All the cushions and throws blend beautifully with antique or contemporary textiles and furniture.

Ceramic tableware
Anta's original ceramics complement the fabrics. From a traditional dinner service to bowls and vases, the ceramics are handmade and hand-decorated with tartans and Scottish flowers.

Flooring
Carpets in traditional flat weaves in pure wool can be fitted or custom-made for rugs or runners and edged with wool binding. There is also a range of hand-decorated and plain-glazed stoneware and tiles.

And finally fashion...
Fashion accessories feature a stylish collection of wool and tweed luggage, handbags, scarves, kilts and ties.

Equestrian Print Room fabric, green; Inset, anticlockwise from top: Equestrian & Classical Garden Print Room Collection; Classical Garden Print Room fabric, yellow; Classical Garden Print Room Toile fabric, charcoal

ARC Collections Limited

Over the past 20 years ARC Collections has become a specialist source of classical prints for galleries, interior designers and the general public. Seventeenth- and eighteenth-century engravings, avidly collected by travellers on a Grand Tour of Europe, were often displayed in print rooms in private houses. Inspired by these highly decorative arrangements of prints, ARC has drawn on its own archive of engravings to create a collection of print room fabric, wallpaper and borders.

There are three designs in the Print Room Collection. Firstly, there is the Classical Garden Print Room, featuring engravings of vases from the gardens of Roman villas by Aquila, vases from Roman palaces by Piranesi, and the statues of Diana and Earth from the gardens of Versailles by Charles Le Brun. Secondly, there is the Equestrian Print Room, featuring Baron d'Eisenberg's beautiful illustrations of the Haute Ecole from the Spanish Riding School, taken from the original paintings at Wilton House in the collection of the Earl of Pembroke. Lastly, ARC presents the French Furniture Print Room, designed to bring to mind a soft, faded French boudoir. This delightful design features beautiful eighteenth-century engravings of luxurious French chairs, beds and sofas.

These stunning designs are available in a wide range of colours, accompanied by hand-printed wallpaper, borders and coordinates. Books, hangers, returnable samples and cuttings are available on request. Retail prices start from £34 plus VAT per metre.

Contact Details

ARC Collections Limited
1 Andrew Place
London
SW8 4RA
Tel: 020 7720 1628
Fax: 020 7622 6214
Email: sales@arccollections.com
Website: www.arccollections.com

From a floral collection to a new take on tartan, a room can be brought to life with beautiful fabrics based on Roger Woods' unique watercolour designs.

Ariadne produces unusual contemporary or classic collections drawn from the unique and beautiful archive of watercolour designs and studies by the artist Roger Woods.

Light and Shade is a collection of watercolour florals that are freely painted and printed on silk, linen and cotton. They are perfect for rooms leading onto the garden, and they can transform a dull room in a town house into an instant conservatory. Prices range from £70 to £90 (RRP).

Alternative Tartan is a range of contemporary silks and silk linens. Woven to order by an English mill established in the eighteenth century, they are both durable and luxurious. These checks are a fresh take on that perennial favourite: the tartan. Derived from watercolour designs, they are a perfect accompaniment to Light and Shade. There is a stunning monochrome palette plus a range of luminous cool and warm shades. A bespoke colouring service is available. Prices range from £70 to £128 (RRP).

Of special note is the collection for gentlemen in linens and cottons, featuring feathers, horses and grasses. Prices range from £48 to £55 (RRP 2006).

Trade and retail enquiries are welcome.

Ariadne

Contact Details

Ariadne Prints, Papers, Weaves
PO Box 208
East Sussex
TN38 0DS
Tel: 01424 423789
Fax/voicemail: 01424 445508
Email: info@ariadneppw.com
Website: www.ariadneppw.com

Above: Cool...rich. Alternative Tartan. English silks (Hercules in mixed media by Roger Woods);
Right: Luxe...calme. Lily from the Light and Shade print collection. Humming Check on chair

Atmosphere

This specialist importer and distributor of double-width textiles from France and Belgium has two shops in England, one in Bath and a new shop in London.

Serving both retail and trade customers since 1994, Atmosphere imports high-quality printed and woven furnishing fabrics directly from a small number of mills in Europe. The product range, which is all available by the roll, comprises classic toiles and florals, contemporary cotton and linen weaves, checks and ginghams, stripes and voiles in a huge variety of designs and colourways.

Ann Cox, the Belgian-born owner, travels regularly to her suppliers, ensuring that the collection remains current and up to the minute in terms of designs, colours and textures.

Extra width
The 280cm width allows the use of the material in unusual and different applications. The extra-wide fabric, which provides twice the normal quantity at minimal extra cost, reduces pattern repeats and making up costs. It can be used for bedspreads, tablecloths and walling fabric, as well as curtains, blinds and upholstery, without the need for joins. Retail prices range from £24 to £39 per metre for the double width.

All product is held in stock on rolls in the store, but can also be viewed on www.atmospherelondon.com. Samples and fabric may be ordered through the website or by telephone or fax, and a mail order service is available.

The company also offers general advice on interior design and soft furnishings, as well as a comprehensive measuring and making up service for all items.

Opposite: unusual toile de Jouy, Villa Borghese, which comes in 280cm width and in two colours black/ecru and red/ecru

Contact Details

Atmosphere Ltd
42 Abbeville Road
London SW4 9NG
Tel/Fax: 020 8673 2440
Email: anncox@atmospherelondon.com
Website: www.atmospherelondon.com

The Percy Bass Decorator's Guide

G P & J Baker

More than a century of discerning collecting has produced one of the most exciting and largest privately owned textile archives in the world.

Founded in 1884 by brothers George Percival and James Baker, G P & J Baker has been producing beautiful prints and weaves for over 100 years. Designs from the company's extensive archive are skilfully adapted to meet with today's transitional tastes and colour palettes and are complemented by luxurious and eclectic weaves.

Today, in addition to developing its own traditional style and unique 'handwriting', G P & J Baker continues to grow its reputation as one of the world's innovators of fabric design and colour. As a holder of the royal warrant, G P & J Baker provides fabrics which are used in royal residences throughout the UK.

Contact Details

G P & J Baker
Chelsea Harbour Design Centre
North Dome G18/19
London SW10 0XE
Tel: 020 7351 7760
Fax: 020 7351 7752

Head Office:
6 Stinsford Road
Poole
Dorset BH17 0SW
Tel: 01202 266700
Fax: 01202 266701
Email: sales@gpjbaker.com
Website: www.gpjbaker.com

Rose de Lamballe

The Beaudesert fabric collection is based on original antique archive documents, unashamedly in the grand tradition, reflecting classical and romantic floral motifs. Characterful figurative prints and historic toiles de Jouy are also a speciality.

Most designs in the collection are hand-printed on a choice of three extremely fine, specially sourced ground cloths – lustrous silk taffeta, crisp slubby linen and a smooth French percale from Lyon. Single colour designs can also come in a delicate polycotton voile.

Managing director Andrew Ginger has spent some ten years building the company's archive, largely eighteenth- and nineteenth-century French in origin and botanical in character. 'The French textile industry from 1850 to 1900 was at its absolute peak of artistic perfection,' he explains. 'The artists employed by fabric houses in this period were extraordinarily gifted. Our challenge is to live up to their standards using modern hand-printing methods. I am often drawn to a design simply for the quality of its artwork, and the challenge of bringing it back to life.'

Some of the more complex romantic patterns have up to 21 individual colours, which are carefully overprinted to make the great depth of tone and sophistication apparent in the designs. 'Rose de Lamballe' has an amazing finesse about it because of the detail in the original artwork. The final printed effect is often compared to painted porcelain.

Other designs are simpler, in a fresh contemporary palette, proving that the collection is not tied to traditional applications alone.

Exquisite antique archive designs are being given new life through hand-printing specialist Beaudesert. The quality and integrity of artwork in each design makes the collection uniquely covetable by those who have discovered it.

Beaudesert

Clockwise, from above right: Rambouillet; Le Bocage; Polo; Clematis Superba

Contact Details

Beaudesert
Old Imperial Laundry
Warriner Gardens
Battersea
London
SW11 4XW
Tel: 020 7720 4977
Fax: 020 7720 4970
Email: info@beaudesert.co.uk
Website: www.beaudesert.co.uk

The Percy Bass Decorator's Guide

Creating a range of original and top-quality products for the world of interior design, this company combines traditional and contemporary styles to produce truly individual pieces.

Beaumont & Fletcher

Beaumont & Fletcher is a specialist company, creating products of the very highest quality for the interior design world that encompass fabrics, wallpapers, traditionally upholstered furniture and hand-carved mirrors and wall-lights.

The fabrics and wallpapers have a very individual look. They range from opulent printed velvets and delicate faded prints to richly woven silks and elegant linens. Beaumont & Fletcher has recently brought out a collection of unique fabrics, entirely embroidered by hand.

Beaumont & Fletcher's extensive range of upholstered furniture has a distinctively individual style that is very English and combines the best of contemporary and traditional design. Each piece is beautifully crafted entirely by hand, using only the most traditional materials and methods. This skilled craftsmanship, together with meticulous attention to detail and finish, has created a collection of bespoke sofas and chairs of Saville Row quality.

Contact Details

Beaumont & Fletcher
261 Fulham Road
London
SW3 6HY
Tel: 020 7352 5594 (Showroom);
020 7498 2642 (Office)
Email: sales@beaumontandfletcher.com
Website: www.beaumontandfletcher.com

Above left: Spitalfields and Rosewalk, two designs from the Beaumont & Fletcher range, entirely embroidered by hand, available on silk and fine linen backgrounds; Left: Pompadour high back sofa in balthazar velvet, c/w verdigris

Bennett Silks

Supplying a huge range of silk fabrics, woven in the traditional homelands of silk production, China, Thailand and India, Bennett Silks always exceeds clients' expectations.

Founded in 1904, Bennett Silks is one of Britain's oldest silk trading companies with over 100 years of expertise in its field. Still a family run business, Bennett Silks supply fine dupion, taffeta and Jacquard silk fabrics for every aspect of the design, decoration and fashion industries from its headquarters in Stockport, Cheshire.

Silk fabrics are woven in the traditional homelands of silk production, China, Thailand and India, to the exacting standards set by the company. Bennett Silks offer 25 different collections, which encompass classic and modern textures in traditional and modern colour palettes. Prices start from around £15 per metre.

Bennett Silks have supplied fashion quality silk used for costumes in operatic productions and count top couture houses amongst their clients. Many fine buildings in London and stately homes around Britain are graced with silks supplied by Bennett Silks.

Photography Oliver Kratz

Contact Details

Bennett Silks
Crown Royal Park
Higher Hillgate
Stockport
Cheshire
SK1 3HB
Tel: 0161 476 8600
Fax: 0161 480 5385
Email: sales@bennett-silks.co.uk
Website: www.bennett-silks.co.uk

Distributed by Garin 1820
Chelsea Harbour Design centre
Unit 2–9, 2nd floor, south dome
London
SW10 0XE
Tel: 020 7351 6496
Fax: 020 7351 3761

Supplying such auspicious interiors as the Vatican, presidential residences and royal palaces, this Venetian weaver preserves a legacy of using traditional techniques to create beautiful fabrics.

Luigi Bevilacqua since 1700

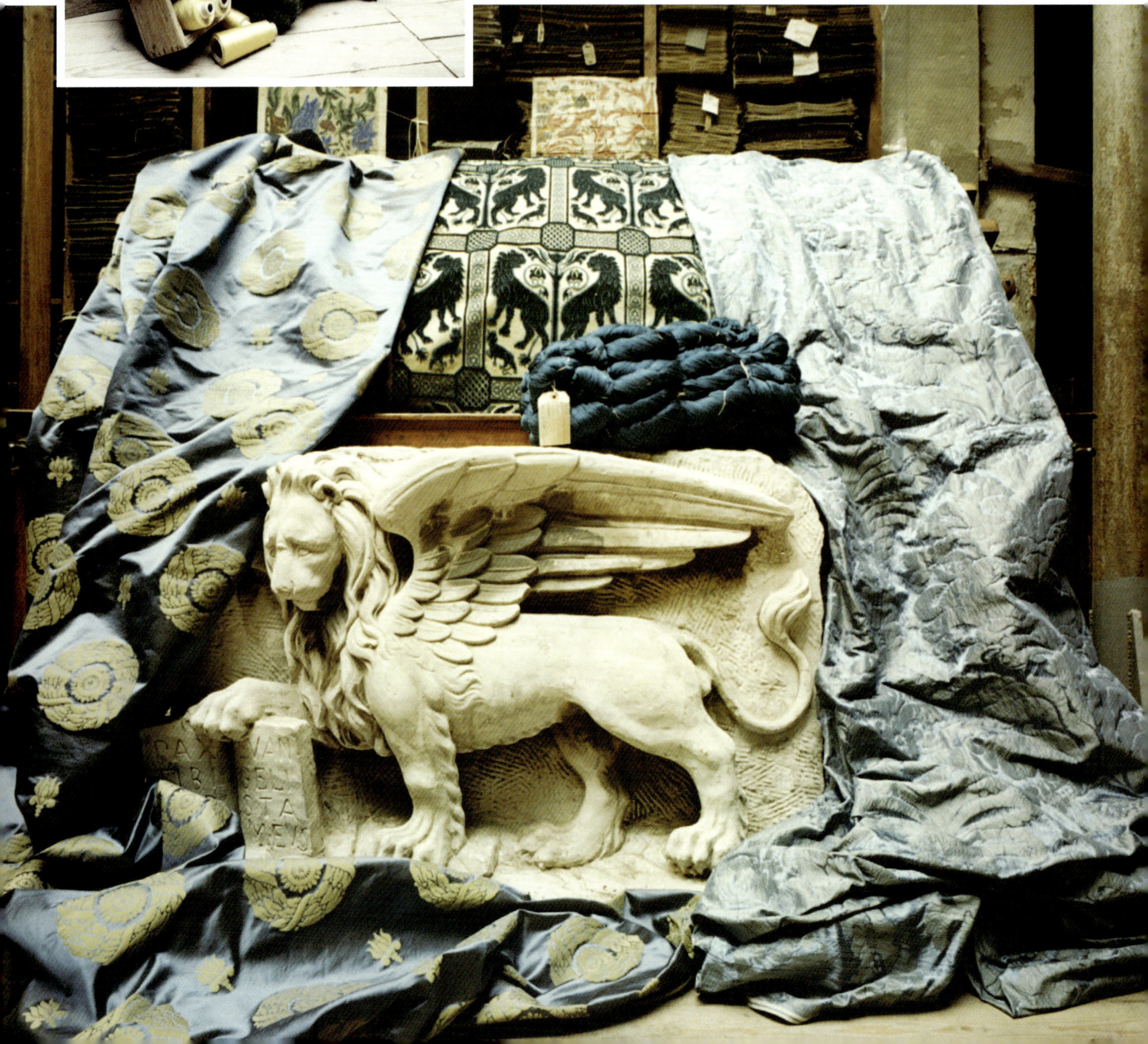

Three centuries ago, Luigi Bevilacqua set up his weaving shop in Venice. Since then, using the same techniques, the same materials and the original eighteenth-century looms, the expert hands of the company's weavers have continued to transform precious natural fibres into soprarizzi velvets, brocades, lampasses, damasks and satins for use in the decoration of palaces, homes and theatres around the world.

Experience and traditions have been passed down from one generation to the next and the company is now in its fourth generation. As a result of this unbroken tradition and the constant dedication to its craft, the company is still using the original techniques of sixteenth-century Venice in the production of its fabrics, helping to preserve the craft of weaving.

Between 1924 and 1926 Bevilacqua was the supplier for the New York company of F. Schumacher & Co, a prestigious firm founded in 1889 which has established itself as a leader in the importation of fine fabrics for the furnishing of interiors.

Bevilacqua was also an official supplier to the Vatican, and its brocades, lampasses and velvets can be seen in some of the main churches of Venice and Rome, among others. It has also provided decorations for the Oval Office in the White House, whose walls are hung with golden yellow worked velvet, the Royal Palace in Sweden, the Casa Rosada in Argentina and the Royal Palace in Kuwait. The company has also worked on several private residences, including cie Palazzo Volpi di Misurata and Palazzo Dario in Venice.

Contact Details

Luigi Bevilacqua srl
Santa Croce 1320
30135 Venezia
Italy
Tel: +39 041 721566
Fax: +39 041 5242302
Email: bevilacqua@luigi-bevilacqua.com
Website: www.luigi-bevilacqua.com

Distributed by Alton-Brooke
Tel: 020 7376 7008

Opposite, from top: A pure silk damask and silk and metal velvet placed on an ancient vertical warping machine; Two silk damasks and one silk soprarizzo velvet on an ancient horizontal warping machine; Above, from left: Velvet 45 Leopardo – tagliato; Velvet 3/3077 Giardino Fioroni – soprarizzo

The Percy Bass Decorator's Guide

Left, (from top): Rippled Hemp Lime; Hand gauffraged silk velvet Turner/Sang Sacré Labrador; Jacquard velvet Top Kapi Pastis

Sabina Fay Braxton

Known for her exuberant extrapolations of ancient hand-printed textile techniques, Sabina Fay Braxton has been creating fabrics for renowned couturiers, interior designers and an array of discriminating private clients for over a decade.

The Sabina Fay Braxton line is an unusual collection of textiles that started in the early 90s, filling a void in the interior textile world. They began as an extrapolation of the medieval technique of gauffrage, creating velvets that had a luminosity and texture that only the passage of time and Fortuny, in his own way, had produced until then. Braxton's invention sprung from the frustration she experienced when designing the interior of a medieval hunting lodge for modern day lifestyle. What resulted was a system that permitted short runs to personalise each space, and was no longer hindered by forbidding minimums on the loom. This had the added bonus of bringing light and life into each textile through the dyeing and printing methods she devised.

Designing concurrently for the haute couture catwalks, working with Lacroix, Valentino, Bill Blass and many others, combined with the influences from her singular childhood travelling remote corners of the globe, has contributed to enriching the collection. The challenge of producing new designs twice a year fed the repertoire and led to new inventions on silk, linen, suede, leather and even vinyl.

While the textiles began as a bespoke service for couture, film and interior, little by little a structured line was formed. The hand-dyed and gauffraged section, comprising some 60 motifs that span from traditional damasks to more abstract textures on some 90 hues of velvet, became known as 'Les Extraordinaires'. The silk

The Percy Bass Decorator's Guide

Right (from top):
Jacquard velvet Ecorce
Brooke; Reliefed linen
Circles Natural

velvets are hand-dyed, giving them a marbled effect and a luminosity and durability that industrial methods cannot achieve. The pile can then be sculpted and encrusted with metals and inks. The silks and linens create a crisper effect and are pressed into bas-reliefs creating a magical effect, like a pronounced watermark, that stands up to being upholstered.

Recently a more informal collection was created: The Braxton Collection with a champagne chic air. Here the fibres used have a more rugged appeal while still retaining the same unpredictable character inherent to the look. Rough hemps are locked into a wrinkled effect and Jacquard velvets are worn down to their tapestry grounds with imperceptibly faint traces of antique gold.

Recent appearances on screen have been in the form of cloaks and office drapes for Richard Harris as Dumbledore in Harry Potter and Klimtesque robes and curtains for Catherine Deneuve, while in the real world the textiles have played prominent roles in hotels such as Aman Jenna, the Parc Hyatt in Milan and the Lancaster in Paris, in addition to the reception rooms of influential potentates.

A home accessories collection is launched twice a year in the form of cushions, throws, fur-backed bedspreads and albums. This brings the vast galaxy of patterns, hues and textures into a coherent whole telling a different story each season.

The line is represented in the UK by Alton-Brooke.

Contact Details

Sabina Fay Braxton
distributed by Alton-Brooke
2–25 Chelsea Harbour Design Centre
Lots Road, London SW10 0XE
Tel: 020 7376 7008
Fax: 020 7376 7009
Email: info@alton-brooke.co.uk
Website: www.alton-brooke.co.uk

A beautiful collection of Textiles inspired by Sally Baring's own archive make for a very personal and elegant look.

Borderline

Borderline was started by Sally Baring with the idea of selling paper and fabric borders, hence the name. Over the years it has evolved into a company selling full-width fabric prints, some weaves and wallpapers. The borders are relegated to the attic!

The collection is now an eclectic mix, including designs from 1730 right up to the present day.

Opposite: Le Chevalier is a French design taken from a document and printed on a heavy linen. Quirky and fun, it is suitable for upholstery or curtains;
Above (top to bottom): Barnaby Stripe was woven for Borderline and comes in two colours.

Le Chevalier Stripe was woven to co-ordinate with Le Chevalier and comes in four colours; Eastern elegance: The Persian print comes from an old quilt in Sally Baring's collection. Some vignettes have been taken from the overall original design which was tiny, enlarged and then pulled apart to give it a more modern look. It is called Oriental Garden; The yellow image of stylised flowers comes off an Indian wedding canopy block printed in gold on silk. It is called Golden Poppy

The Percy Bass Decorator's Guide

Japanese Floral, Japanese Bamboo and Ikeda are all printed on fabric or paper, including gold and silver mylar

Left: An important part of the Borderline collection is the Florence Broadhurst Collection. Designed in the 1960s by a versatile and fascinating individual, the collection includes eastern-influenced elegant designs printed on cotton or cotton union and wallpapers. The gold image is called Cranes and is one of the most popular wallpapers printed on gold mylar

Contact Details

Borderline
Unit 12, 3rd Floor
Chelsea Harbour Design Centre
London
SW10 0XE
Tel: 020 7823 3567
Fax: 020 7351 7644
Email: sally.baring@borderlinefabrics.com
Website: www.borderlinefabrics.com

Above: Roxy linen in fizzing pink and Boudoir stripe silk in apple; Inset (from top): Pynefrute in ionian blue on white linen; Sylvi silk taffeta in delphinium; Fancy Linen heavy linen weaves; Summer Palace silk damask in eucalyptus colourway

Busby & Busby

Full of design inspiration, this collection consists of an eclectic mix of genuine toiles, fresh linen weaves, flowing brushstrokes and beautiful silks.

Bren Busby is the creative force behind this independent British producer and seeks to inspire people through her designs rather than merely find a solution to a problem. 'Everything we produce must possess integrity, elegance and that "why not" factor,' she insists.

Evolving style
The fabrics illustrated give an excellent cross-section of the Busby style, which is constantly evolving, never static and seeks to bring pleasure to the beholder year after year. Roxy and Boudoir have a vaguely retro style with a charmingly 1950s atmosphere. Pynefrute brings a fluid gracefulness to this traditional symbol of welcome. Summer Palace is Busby's newest and grandest silk damask. Sylvi demonstrates a simple charm in silk taffeta. All fabrics are produced in a choice of colourways.

Although Busby & Busby is hidden away in deepest Dorset, the fabrics grace many a prestigious location and can be sourced through specialist decorators throughout the world.

Contact Details

Busby & Busby
The Old Stables
Winterborne Whitechurch
Dorset
DT11 9AW
Tel: 01258 881211
Fax: 01258 881351
Email: enquiries@busbyfabric.com
Website: www.busbyfabric.com

The Percy Bass Decorator's Guide

Right: Original chair from Charles Rennie Mackintosh covered in an exact reproduction of his horsehair fabric Dales DA/681/1 blue/black; Above: Decorex stand from 2003 showing furniture and lighting from Lutyens Design Associates and wallpanels upholstered in horsehair fabric Paso PA/520 pale brass; Opposite: Decorex stand from 2002 with furniture and lighting from Ochre and wallpanels upholstered in horsehair fabric Paso PA/524 turquoise/grey

First established in 1837 by John Boyd, a Scotsman from Ayrshire, John Boyd Textiles continues the tradition of horsehair weaving in Castle Cary, Somerset, using the original looms and techniques since 1870.

Originally a cottage industry, horsehair fabric was mainly woven by hand at home. By 1851, John Boyd had expanded his business and moved to a purpose-built factory employing 39 staff and 34 children. In 1870, the Education Act ensured that children attended school and this then led to the development of mechanical looms still used today which were patented in 1872. Horsehair fabric was especially popular in Victorian times with a very varied colour palette, not just the plain black associated with upholstery on Victorian antiques today.

There are two widths of horsehair fabrics that are limited to the length of the horse's tail: 26 inches for fabrics woven with black and natural grey hair and 22 inches for fabrics woven with natural white hair. At that time, it was the fashion to crop

John Boyd Textiles

Since 1837, this company has been weaving horsehair fabrics, used mainly for upholstery of antique, traditional and contemporary furniture. Also used for wall coverings and lampshades, this exclusive natural English fabric is highly regarded for its quality, durability and lustre.

horses' tails and also working horses', to ensure that the tails did not become tangled in farm ploughs and machinery. The horsehair must be taken from live horses, just like wool from sheep, to ensure the strength and vitality of the hair for weaving.

Famous designers
Horsehair fabric was originally used by great furniture designers such as Thomas Chippendale, George Hepplewhite, Sir Edwin Lutyens and Charles Rennie Mackintosh. Thomas Chippendale specified striped horsehair fabric as the classic dining chair fabric and Mackintoch used the sateen weave and a small blue check weave on the Argyle Tea Room chairs.

All the classic designs and colours are still woven today on the original looms. In addition to these fabrics, many new weaves and contemporary colours have been added to the range and used by more contemporary designers such as David Collins and Spencer Fung Architects for upholstery and wall coverings in modern settings. John Boyd Textiles also offers the service of embroidering any design onto horsehair fabric.

Retail prices from £100 per metre from retail outlets such as Percy Bass.

Contact Details

John Boyd Textiles
Higher Flax Mills
Castle Cary
Somerset
BA7 7DY
Tel: 01963 350451
Fax: 01963 351078
Email: enquiries@johnboydtextiles.co.uk
Website: www.johnboydtextiles.co.uk

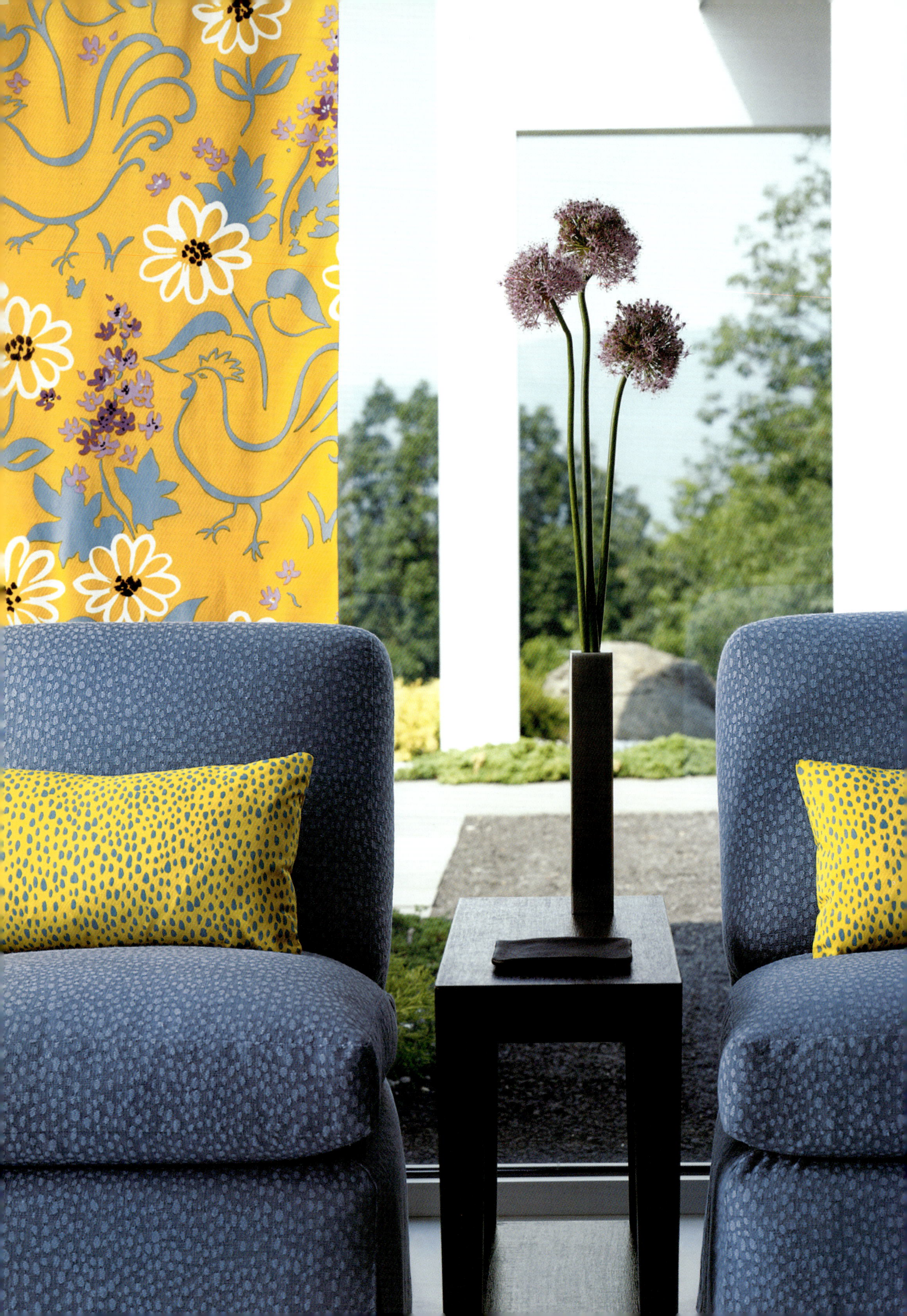

Opposite: Hugues Capet Cotton Print (curtains), La Pluie Woven Texture (on Baltimore chairs), La Pluie Cotton Print (on pillows), Tribeca slim table; Right: On the Rialto chair is the sumptuous cut velvet Angles in the tradition of Art Deco/Art Moderne… with an occasional salute to the twentieth-century artists Kandinsky and Miro

The classic/modern Kirk Brummel Collection reflects the style and luxury of the 1960s, whereas the Paule Marrot Editions have the sophisticated simplification of impressionistic Paris.

Brunschwig & Fils

The Kirk Brummel Collection of fine woven textiles – a division of Brunschwig & Fils worldwide – comprises over 80 designs under the artistic direction of Michael Brummel, an American designer who began building his vision of style and luxury in New York in the late 1960s. Brummel's travels took him to Vienna, where he was influenced by the Secessionists and Wiener Werkstatte and to Paris, where he was inspired by the work of the International Modernists.

Visually and technically innovative, these designs combine bold abstract patterns with unusual colours, resulting in fabrics that are a delight to the eye and warm to the touch. Woven in mills around the world, they favour natural fibres such as linen, silk and cotton, at times integrating the addition of mixed constructions for strength and textural interest. There is a lot here to please the architect and interior designer.

Parisian motifs
Brunschwig & Fils received permission from the Paule Marrot Estate to produce the designs that Madame Marrot designed in the early part of the twentieth century. Paule Marrot lived in France from 1902 to 1987 and had a great influence on textile design. In turn, her designs reflected the trends of twentieth-century art toward sophisticated simplification, as exemplified in the work of such artists as Matisse, Cézanne and Dufy. Marrot's fresh primary colours and the simple forms of her motifs – flowers, butterflies, forests, meadows and birds – charmed a generation. She changed the way people saw colour and form. By 1919 she was already printing designs on fabric and in 1922 she exhibited her textiles at the Salon des Artistes Décorateurs in Paris. By 1932, she was printing her designs professionally in a mill in Alsace. In 1952 Paule Marrot received the Legion of Honour for her contribution to textile design in France.

Contact Details

Brunschwig & Fils
10, The Chambers
Chelsea Harbour Drive
London
SW10 0XF
Tel: 020 7351 5797
Fax: 020 7351 2280
Email: staff@brunschwig.com
Website: www.brunschwig.com

Hatley Lilac bedding printed onto Egyptian cotton; Inset: Mary Blue cushion on Tea Stained linen; Above right: Mary Lilac wallpaper, Kate Lilac cushion on Tea Stained Linen, Vintage Stripey cushion

Cabbages & Roses designs and produces an exclusive range of clothes, gifts and an ever-expanding range of household items. The faded vintage-inspired fabrics are all hand-printed in England and include antique linen sheets and a range of Irish linen fabrics in Cabbages & Roses designs.

The company is introducing a bed linen collection in 2005, printed with Hatley Rose. A small stock of vintage and antique furniture, accessories, quilts and china is also available from Cabbages & Roses shops.

Contact Details

Cabbages & Roses
3 Langton Street
London
SW10 0JL
Tel: 020 7352 7333
Website: www.cabbagesandroses.com

Classic in style, contemporary in application and offering a vast array of household items, clothes and gifts, this very English company has something to suit all tastes.

Cabbages & Roses

Sleek, tailored, silk designs in unique colours have succeeded in making Chase Erwin an international boutique-style fabric house. This modern company is favoured by top interior designers, exclusive hotels and luxury yacht owners worldwide.

Chase Erwin

Confident colours, subtle weaves and rich textures are what make Chase Erwin silks so unique. Ragna, an Icelandic national, creates stunning designs that reflect her wild yet tranquil native landscape of glaciers, fjords, waterfalls and mountains.

This year's innovative new collection, Aviaya, complements the existing designs, capturing the diversity and complexity of light and shade in clean fresh colours. Aviaya, meaning 'little flower' in the Eskimo language, aptly conveys the icy beauty of frost roses on windows, which inspired the collection of silk taffetas, silk velvets, pure silk chenille, and beautiful silk damask.

The popular Diva range comprises over 70 stunning colours in shimmering two-ply silk. These versatile unadorned silks balance the striking array of patterned silks offered by Chase Erwin. The designs include nautical checks, stripes and cubes, textured ribs, classic hand-printed motifs, and contemporary weaves that are highly regarded on the interior design market.

The opaque silks are enhanced by a variety of delicate silk organza sheers, hand embroidered with tiny beads and silk thread in India. These diverse collections are completed by an impressive range of upholstery fabrics, including faux-suede, the softest kid mohair and luxurious silk velvet, textured linen, silk viscose blends, raffia and chenille.

Whilst establishing a reputation as a leading specialist in silks, the company has remained small and personal. Chelsea Harbour Design Centre is home to Chase Erwin's elegant showroom, and the distribution of fabrics takes place in a chic 1950s redbrick warehouse on the south side of the river Thames.

Contact Details

Chase Erwin Silk
22 Chelsea Harbour Design Centre
London
SW10 0XE
Tel: 020 8875 1222
Email: silk@chase-erwin.com
Website: www.chase-erwin.com

Below: Silk, with real silk chinelle in the horizontal stripe; Inset, from top: The vertical stripes of the new Riva, in dragon and copper; Pleated Sirena silk in copper and one of many upholstery lines introduced by Chase Erwin, Cirrus Snow

Right: Ocre flower & fern; Below: Furniture, Side Table Gus 80/0 Antique Gray, Oval Back Chair Gus 10/0 Antique Gray

Contact Details

Chelsea Textiles
Textile Showroom
7 Walton Street
London
SW3 2JD
Tel: 020 7584 0111
Fax: 020 7584 7170
Email: sales@chelsea-textiles.co.uk
Website: www.chelseatextiles.com

All Chelsea Textiles fabric designs are taken from original antique documents of the seventeenth, eighteenth and nineteenth centuries, with nearly all designs originating from England or France. The fabric range goes from the late seventeenth-century Jacobean to early nineteenth-century Empire with a dash of William Morris from the late nineteenth-century, but the most concentrated period of embroidery is Queen Anne and Louis XVI.

In addition, each client is offered a unique personalised service. Chelsea Textiles can accommodate customers' personal requirements, be it specific colourways or made-to-measure panels.

Chelsea Textiles is renowned for its ability to replicate antique furniture designs so exact as to be indistinguishable from the pieces that inspired them. The Gustavian collection is all handmade to traditional specifications, hand-painted and hand-distressed in an authentic antique colour palette. The simple lines and subtle colours of Swedish Gustavian furniture blend well with the natural interiors currently in vogue, and now so avidly sought after.

Chelsea Textiles also offers a beautiful collection of home accessories, which includes classic needlepoint cushions to coordinate with the textiles.

Chelsea Textiles

Established in 1991, Chelsea Textiles is well known for its expertise in recreating exquisite designs from precious remnants of antique cloth found in auctions, attics and armoires from around the world. Meticulous research and an insistance on the use of authentic materials are in evidence in the textile house's hand-embroidered collection, which incorporates over 200 designs, with around 100 backing fabrics including checks and ticking.

Natural texture and originality in versatile and timeless crewel fabrics

Coromandel Crafts Ltd.

Coromandel is a long-established family company with a reputation for offering exclusive, hand-embroidered crewel and handloom fabric of outstanding quality at an affordable price. In business since 1978, the company is one of the most experienced importers of crewel and supplies many top interior designers. It aims to provide clients with natural, elegant and luxurious fabrics, which will add an instant and timeless appeal to any design scheme.

Reflecting its early English heritage, Coromandel crewel is commissioned in specific designs. The multi-coloured designs feature carefully selected tones, which are particularly stunning in juxtaposition with original features such as wood panelling, stonework or oak beams. The naturals combine classic simplicity and elegance with texture and originality. Given a hidden dimension at certain times of day, when suffused with sunlight filtering through the embroidery, the cream on cream crewel is extremely versatile, working well in both traditional and modern schemes.

Complementing the crewel, Coromandel handlooms have the same natural feel as linen. Used in combination with the embroidered fabric, they provide an economical alternative to schemes using just crewel and they also provide a sympathetically textured lining.

Finished products include hand-crafted furniture such as stools, linen baskets, waste paper bins and lampshades, as well as hand-finished soft furnishings. A bespoke service also offers the possibility of commissioning a one-off piece in any of Coromandel's fabrics.

As customers become increasingly aware of environmental impact, and as it consists of 100 per cent wool hand-embroidery on 100 per cent handloom cotton, the crewel provides a natural and cost-effective alternative to mass-produced, synthetic fabrics. Coromandel offers a competent service with a high regard for detail, ensuring prompt dispatch of returnable samples and orders to all clients. Prices range from £12 per metre for handloom and from £35 to £45 per metre for crewel fabric.

Contact Details

Coromandel Crafts Ltd.
Heatherbell
Tintagel Road
Finchampstead
Berkshire
RG40 3JJ
Tel: 0118 979 6222
Fax: 0118 979 6888
Email: pbsales@coromandel.co.uk
Website: www.coromandel.co.uk

The Percy Bass Decorator's Guide

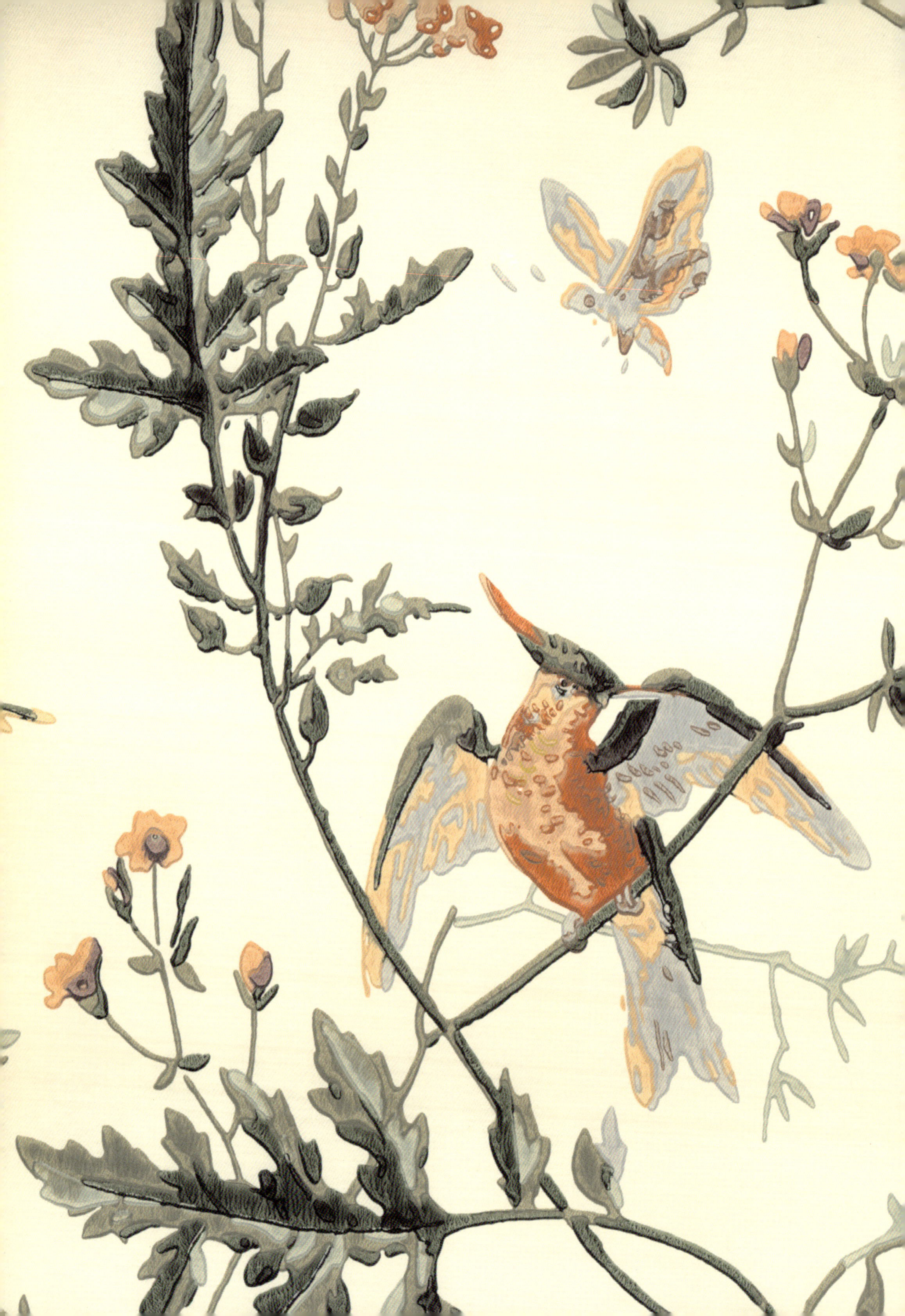

Opposite: Humming Birds 66/1001;
Right, from top: Malabar 66/1007;
Woodstock 69/7128; Woods 69/12147

Cole & Son

From producing custom-made wallpapers on antiquated machinery to the latest contemporary wallpaper designs, this company has over 100 years of experience in the wallpaper industry. It is, however, best known for its beautiful flock wallpapers that are a feature of the Houses of Parliament and the Lord Chancellor's apartment.

The wallpaper business of Cole & Son was established in 1873, but inherited an archive of hand-carved printing blocks dating back to 1750. This enables Coles to draw on a unique historical source when creating new design ranges. The company regularly supplies customised wallpapers from its blocks for landmark properties, including Buckingham Palace, Balmoral Castle and The White House.

New collections of wallpapers are regularly produced from archive material. An eighteenth-century design called Hummingbird is taken from an original section of a block print. This design has matching fabric and is made in four colourways, with its oriental-inspired design proving very popular.

Recently, the emphasis has been on contemporary designs from the 1950s and the 1960s. These have been re-coloured for modern tastes and include geometric designs by David Hicks. Another award-winning, unusual design is sketched from trees and branches making a unique repeat. This dates from 1959 and has also been re-coloured. As a tribute to the swinging sixties, the psychedelic Woodstock design, with metallic swirls, complements the current furniture design styles, as does the 1960s design Malabar.

This is a company which specialises in the highest quality wallpapers, from the best-selling Florence collection to the very latest in contemporary design.

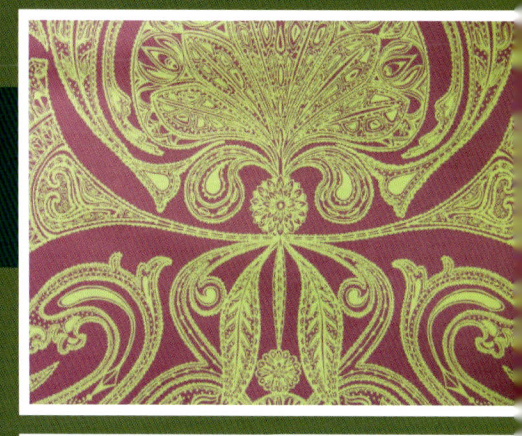

Contact Details

Cole & Son (Wallpapers) Ltd
G10, Chelsea Harbour Design Centre
Lots Road
London
SW10 0XE
Tel: 020 7376 4628
Fax: 020 7376 4631
Email: raema.cook@cole-and-son.com
Website: www.cole-and-son.com

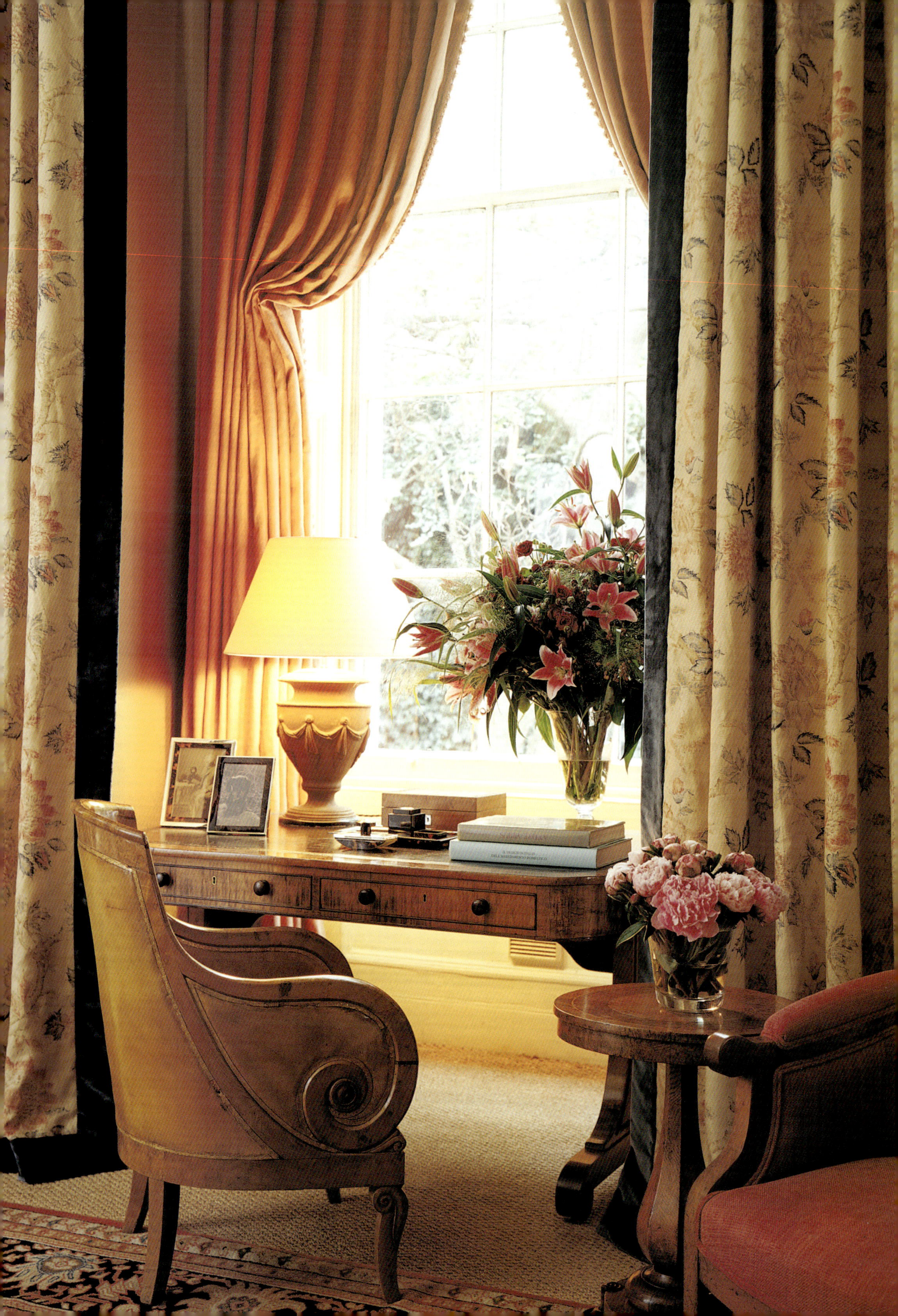

Colefax and Fowler

For discerning individuals looking for sheer excellence, true refinement and, most important of all, deep comfort in their home, Colefax and Fowler is unquestionably Mecca.

The essence of design
As the very essence of Englishness, the name of Colefax and Fowler has always been synonymous with timeless design. Colefax and Fowler epitomise what has come to be recognised as English style – a style which is admired and emulated across the world. This English look combines elegance and subtlety with real comfort, every element being of the highest quality. Today, modern interiors, like modern life, are rather more informal, more relaxed than they were in the past and Colefax and Fowler's present day collections, with their understated colours and designs reflect this warm easier feeling.

Beautiful prints
The Colefax and Fowler tradition of excellence is demonstrated in the design and manufacturing of every new collection. As in the past, most of the designs in the new collections are based on, or inspired by 19th century document prints from the company's archives, but each one has been interpreted for today. The design, which takes between 12 and 18 months to develop, is reworked and re-coloured by the design team. It is then printed onto the chosen textile, using a complex printing process which necessitates using separate screens for every colour; each new shade is layered one over another, giving subtleties and gradations of tone which make Colefax and Fowler prints immediately recognisable. Among the recent collections a soft textured combination of linen and cotton predominates.

The inspirational colours range from the subtle to the soft: understated tones like aubergine, lilac, charcoal and coral, or the softened palette of raspberry pinks, milky blues and leafy greens.

Luxurious weaves
Colefax and Fowler are deservedly famous for their wide range of textiles, woven in leading European mills and Asia. Made to the highest standard, these luxurious weaves include velvet, chenille and wool; silk and embroidery and rustic, informal weaves. The colours, as befits these rich textures, glow and shimmer with the light include: amethyst, gold and terracotta; tomato, ivory and sienna; sand and claret.

Elegant wallpapers
As with their exclusive fabric designs, Colefax and Fowler wallpapers reflect the elegance and style of the classic interior. Based on English and French 18th and 19th century documents, designs include decorative florals, motifs, stripes and paint effects. Some of the papers are surface-printed to emulate hand-blocking techniques which gives greater definition to the design.

Today, the market maybe worldwide, and the collection far larger than when John Fowler first designed special fabrics for his decorating clients, but his legacy of uncompromising excellence means that the Colefax and Fowler name continues to be synonymous with good design and superlative quality, as well as a determination to offer only the very best fabrics and wallpapers.

From top: chair - Eskdale Check, cushion - Tarn; curtain - Darsham & Polidoro; Opposite: curtain - Darsham, chair - Tarn

Contact Details
Colefax and Fowler
Tel: 020 8874 6484
Fax: 020 8877 0064
Website: www.colefax.com

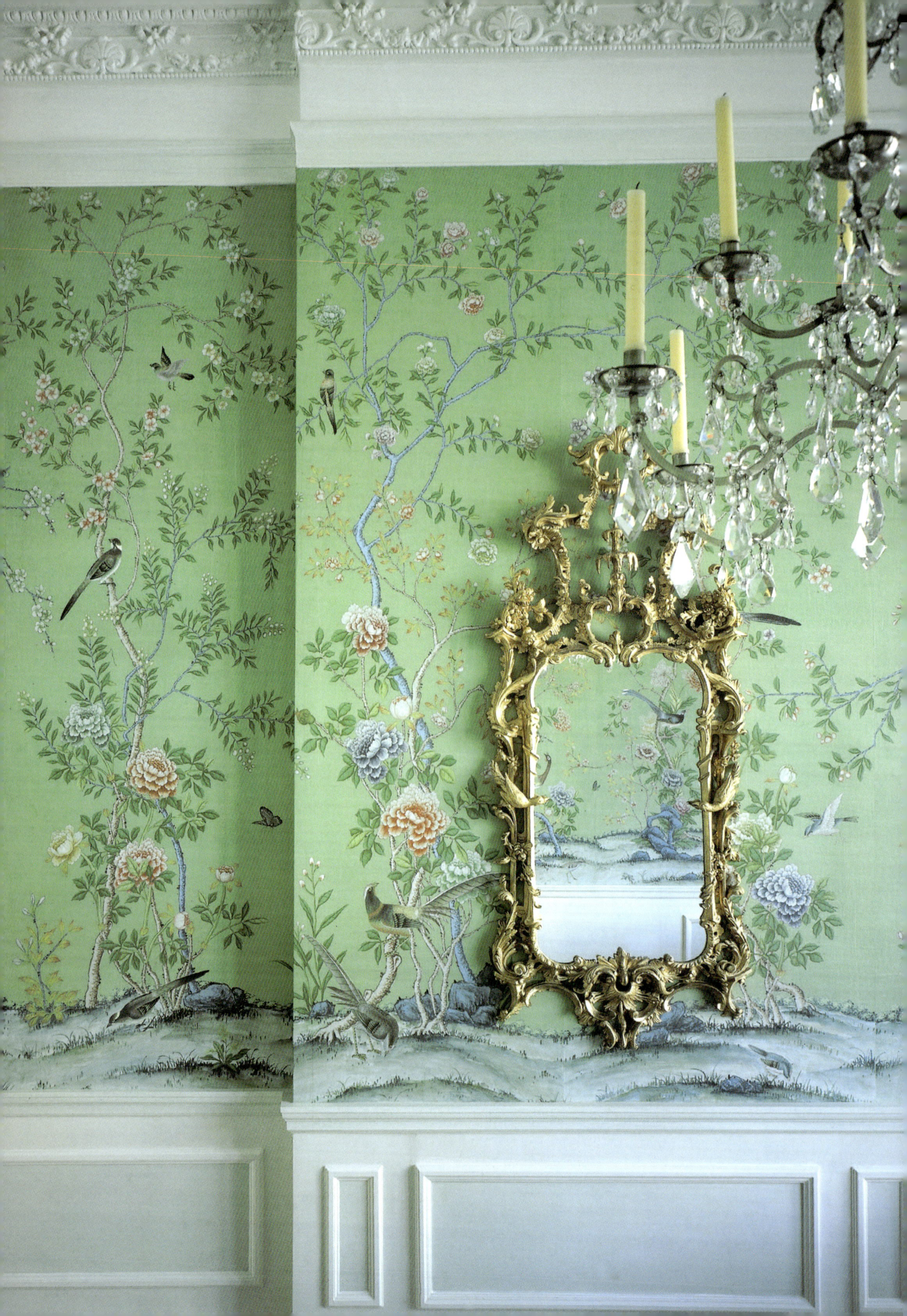

de Gournay was created in 1984 by Claud Cecil-Gurney to revive the art of hand-painting Chinoiserie wallpapers in China. From the outset the company was intent on faithfully reproducing eighteenth-century originals and adapting the designs to become more relevant for use in contemporary interiors. Currently, de Gournay undertakes projects for most of the world's leading heritage bodies as well as many top designers and couturiers.

de Gournay established the first western-owned porcelain company in Jingdezhen to produce copies of eighteenth-century armorial dinner services and figurines. It has completed dinner services for many grand old families and also produced contemporary designs to suit more modern tastes. de Gournay believes its copies are the best currently available; indeed they are frequently mistaken as originals and sold as such by auction houses around the world.

All production is carried out in the company's own studios by its own personnel. de Gournay has a complete understanding of the techniques and materials that have been used over the centuries and is in a unique position to offer its own designs or work to designs specified by clients. Over the years de Gournay has built up an extensive database of originals and copies and is happy to share this database with clients who are trying to create a unique wallpaper or dinner service.

de Gournay has broadened its range of products from Chinoiserie wallpapers to include reproductions of nineteenth-century French Papiers Peints Panoramiques, and it can produce any designs not still produced by the original firms in France, as well as new designs.

All de Gournay designs are also produced as fabrics and can be adapted for use as curtains, bed covers and upholstery materials as required. Wallpapers can be manufactured as fabrics that can be stretched onto the walls instead of being hung. de Gournay also produces finished blinds to any size, either in plain fabrics or using any of its designs. These can be on sheers/organzas or on opaque materials as required.

If you wish to create a Chinoiserie room, de Gournay offers a complete service in the production of wallpapers, fabrics and porcelain. Equally, if you wish to use just some elements of Chinoiserie or Papiers Peints Panoramiques in your design, de Gournay will be happy to quote for your wallpaper, curtains or blinds as required.

Contact Details

de Gournay
112 Old Church Street
Chelsea
London SW3 6EP
Tel: 020 7823 7316
Fax: 01892 871040
Email: info@degournay.com
Website: www.degournay.com

de Gournay

Whether you want a complete Chinoiserie room as at the Brighton Pavilion, or to introduce elements of Chinoiserie or Papiers Peints Panoramiques into your design, this company has the wallpapers, fabrics, porcelain, curtains or blinds for you.

The Percy Bass Decorator's Guide

The Percy Bass Decorator's Guide

Designers Guild, a contemporary way of life

Opposite: Coromandel silk curtain in acacia; Inset, from top: China Rose ecru – Scoop sofa in Saraceno linen, Scoop chair in Caterina raven, Curtains in China Rose ecru; China Rose Cassis – Square Sofa in Cordelina peony Curtains in China Rose cassis and Francia poppy, Square sofa in Zilleri peony, Antique stool covered in Pavlovsk crocus; Coromandel silk in sienna with Connaught Place in sienna; Above: Imperialis Sepia – Details of curtains in Rosalina sand and natural. Cushion in Morskaya linen

Mixing the contemporary with comfort, and introducing an extraordinary array of textiles and fabrics into its collections, Designers Guild has managed to establish itself as one of the most respected interior design companies in the world.

Tricia Guild founded Designers Guild in London in 1970 and it has since grown to become one of the most influential and creative forces in the world of interior design. The company has achieved international renown for a wide variety of home and lifestyle products; most notably, innovative furnishing fabrics and wallpapers, bed and bath, furniture, and collections of paint, carpets and rugs. The company also produces a range of stationery and accessories and the Fragrant Home collection of scented candles and room sprays. In short, Designers Guild provides almost everything one needs to make a room a home rather than just a designed space.

Under Tricia Guild's creative direction, the company has built up a broad base of products that have a wide variety of uses. Although it is widely known for its use of bright colour, the company in fact offers an extraordinary array of textiles and wall coverings. From richly decorative floral prints to cool neutral weaves, from brightly coloured velvet stripes and silks to more classical damasks and cut velvets, and from modern geometric prints in monochrome black and white to beautifully embellished flocked silks, linens and faux suede, Designers Guild really does have a huge selection.

As well as the extensive collection for adults, the company also has a fabulous collection for kids.

The Designers Guild business philosophy is to combine creativity and innovation with the highest levels of quality: quality of design, product, service and people.

Contact Details

Designers Guild
Showroom and Homestore
267–277 Kings Road
London
SW3 5EN
Tel: 020 7351 5775
Email: info@designersguild.com
Website: www.designersguild.com

The Percy Bass Decorator's Guide

Registered as a Rialto Trader in 1090, Ioannes Donatus set sail for the Near East to import marvellous Byzantine fabrics. Ioannes was an ancestor of the Venetian Donà dalle Rose family which, since their origins around the year 1000, was immensely active in fervent trading with the magical Orient.

Today, his descendants have decided to bring out the most enchanting décors from the paintings, 'sampling' this classical vocabulary to create contemporary fabrics that have the textures and patinas of the old ones, without their fatal fragility. They are inspired by Paolo Veneziano, Vivarini, Fr. Angelico, Bellini, and, more specifically, the painted robes of Venetian dignitaries and Doges.

Inspirational collections
The Donatus Cinquecento Collection is presented at the Paris Biennale for the first time with a pattern directly drawn from the archives and sampled on linen sergès and silk velvets. Celestial figures, clouds and gold flames, ornamental mysteries are superimposed upon shadowy backgrounds. Symbols and colours, courageously painted in old palazzos, come to life magically.

The times when navigators were discovering the wonders of oriental markets may have now passed, yet the memory of those designs and colours is still alive and ever present.

Donatus

Top left: The Donatus Cinquecento Collection, pomegranates and golden lilies, entangled bunches of grapes, precious stones and painted tiaras discovered on the attire of primitive Madonnas; Opposite, top right: The digital prints of blown up tattoes on silk give a contemporary dimension to ancient archaic signs and representative symbols of ancestral emotions; Opposite, bottom right: The Byzantine Collection, an ancient story of royal eagles and tempestuous lagoons, reverberating water courses, runic symbols and glittering diamond mounts

Contact Details

Donatus Venetian Fabrics
Showroom by appointment
Palazzo Donà
5101 Fondamente Nove
30131 Venezia, Italy
Tel: +39 041 241 06 74
Fax: +39 041 241 54 24
Email: mail@donatus.com
Website: www.donatus.com

Exclusive agent for the UK
Miss Beata von Oelreich
43, St. Stephens Gardens
London, W2 5NA
Tel: 07775 785 744

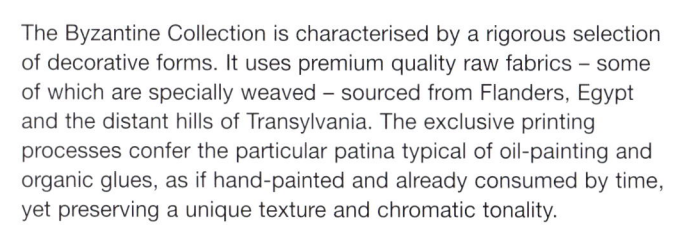

The Byzantine Collection is characterised by a rigorous selection of decorative forms. It uses premium quality raw fabrics – some of which are specially weaved – sourced from Flanders, Egypt and the distant hills of Transylvania. The exclusive printing processes confer the particular patina typical of oil-painting and organic glues, as if hand-painted and already consumed by time, yet preserving a unique texture and chromatic tonality.

Avant garde ideas
Donatus expresses constant innovation. The 'skin fabrics' incorporate ideas from a creative collaboration with avant garde guest artists responding to an irresistible urge to surprise, create and transform the world with instinctive visions.

The careful research carried out by Donatus Venetian Fabrics through years of study and experimentation imparts an original and abstract beauty, coherent with contemporary concepts of interior design.

Prices for hand-printed fabrics range from €85 to €158 per linear metre. For hand-printed, custom-made projects or painted atelier projects price are estimated for each project, but usually range from €80 (simple décors), to €400 per linear metre or square metre (for antique gold-leaf décors or very elaborate drawings).

AD8 and AD9 Acrylic disc tiebacks from the Contemporary collection; Opposite, from top: From the classically inspired Desire collection with custom-made tassel and crystals; Lorenzo damask; Range from the Long Island collection

Jason D'Souza is renowned for his classic fabric collections embellished with a subtle modern edge.

Jason D'Souza

After studying at Chelsea School of Art, Jason began his career in 1990 designing a range of hand printed cushions. These were successfully sold at Harrods and Harvey Nicholls resulting in requests for fabrics. Following on from this, Jason, together with his sister Melina, launched his exclusive ranges at exhibitions such as Decorex before opening his current showroom at Chelsea Harbour.

Today this innovative company concentrates on the top end of the decorating market, producing inspiring textiles for distinctive interiors. The versatile collections encompass sophisticated contemporary fabrics suitable for domestic and contract use. The current Desire range is a sumptuous combination of textures and patterns incorporating classical motifs with contemporary constructions. Exuberant use of colour epitomises this collection fusing a colour palette that includes aqua and taupe, aubergine and lime, teal and chocolate, all ingeniously blended.

For clients seeking a completely inspiring look, there is a range of stamped patent leather in mock croc, ostrich and buffalo, ideal for modern furniture.

To round off the fabrics, alongside a traditional collection, a contemporary range of custom-made tassels and trimmings is also offered. These are finely detailed and include imaginative use of glass, crystals and Perspex.

Contact Details

Jason D'Souza Ltd
1/6 Chelsea Harbour Design Centre
Chelsea Harbour
London
SW10 0XE
Tel: 020 7351 4440
Fax: 020 7351 4396
Email: Info@jasondsouza.co.uk
Website: www.jasondsouza.co.uk

Jim Dickens

With a well established reputation, this fabric wholesaler has created fabrics with a distinctive quality and feel. Inspired by history, nature and art, this collection aims to suit and reflect every customer's needs.

Contact Details

Jim Dickens
64 Britannia Way
Britannia Enterprise Park
Lichfield, Staffordshire
WS14 9UY
Tel: 01543 415588
Fax: 01543 410548
Email: jimdickens@btconnect.com
Website: www.jimdickens.co.uk

Jim Dickens has recently launched its new collection. Based in the heart of Staffordshire, this new fabric brand has established a strong reputation in the world of textiles. Specialising in the highest quality drapes and upholstery fabric, Jim Dickens's designs draw on a range of influences from traditional English culture to Islamic art.

The designs go beyond traditional naturalism by using forms derived from obscure and exotic designs as well as simple and classical elements. The evolutionary design of the collection bears no single approach but is used as a basis for contemporary appeal. Apart from the visual influence, the touch of the fabrics exudes sensuality, which dispels the myth of using different fabrics in drapery and upholstery.

The asymmetric, curvilinear profile and use of floral detailing will be equally at home in country houses as in smart apartments and penthouses. Interiors will blend with aspiration, re-inventing the classical past or reflecting the contemporary. The collection is a means of discovering the soul, the existence of which modern materialism appears to have left behind.

The collection comprises fabrics from individual designers and companies who, resistant to selling abroad, cherish the home market. The designs reflect the new aesthetic diversity across Britain through the remarkable collection.

The company's extremely eclectic style, both in the look of the fabric and the personal service it conveys, give the collection its cohesiveness and significance.

Evertrading Ltd

From the lightest polar bear to the darkest sable and softest chinchilla, this company offers an impressive collection of luxurious faux furs and tabletop accessories, combining contemporary elegance with a romantic twist.

Evertrading has supplied top quality faux fur to prestigious interior designers and retailers since 1995.

The collection includes 12 different faux furs in the highest quality and is flame retardant to hotel standard. The range includes the lightest polar bear to dark trimmed sable. The faux fur matches all the different types of real fur to perfection, from the softest chinchilla to bear. The choice of linings includes a soft cashmere mix in a number of different shades and a gorgeous cotton velvet. The faux furs as well as the linings are regularly being updated with new colours and styles to suit the latest trends in interior design.

Evertrading offers four sizes of faux fur throw, from the standard-size throw to the large king-size bedspread. Also available are cushions in several designs and hot water bottle covers. These sumptuous and luxurious faux furs will add ambience to any contemporary interior and will complement the more traditional home just as well.

Hand-engraved glassware and plain white ceramics are included in Evertrading's tabletop range. Whether designing the range itself or commissioning pieces from leading craftsmen throughout Europe, the criteria are always the same. Each piece needs to be elegant and contemporary, with a sensuous and romantic twist.

Many of the glass designs and decorations are inspired by antique collections, some just as contemporary today as they were in previous centuries. From its unique collection of hand-engraved glassware to its scented hand-decorated candles, each piece is individually made using time-honoured skills. Therefore no two pieces are exactly alike or, in other words, they are all perfectly imperfect.

Contact Details

Evertrading Ltd
12 Martindale
London
SW14 7AL
Tel: 020 8878 4050
Fax: 020 8876 5717
Email: sales@evertrading.co.uk

Above: Faux fur throw, available in 12 different faux furs and many different sizes. Shown here in grey chinchilla, lined with grey velvet; Inset left: Hot water bottle cover shown here in grey chinchilla, bear and polar bear; Inset right: Cushions (from top), grey chinchilla bolster cushion with sides in grey marmot fur trim cushion with beige velvet front and back, fox whole fur front lined with astird rose in honey, Lynx fur front cushion with lining and edge in taupe velvet

Eclipse Carpets

Hand-weaving bespoke rugs using traditional methods, this company offers an extensive range of colours, weaves and sizes to suit and satisfy any requirement.

Above: East Meon, 100 knot
Right: Oliver's Castle, 100 knot
Opposite: Monsoon, 80 knot

Eclipse Carpets wool rugs are made in Kathmandu, Nepal. Each rug is entirely handmade from carding, dyeing, spinning, weaving, cutting washing and drying. Depending on the size, it takes an average of three months from order to delivery.

No child labour is used in the manufacture of Eclipse rugs. In fact, a percentage of the cost of each square metre made is contributed to an educational fund for the children of the weavers.

Each rug is made specifically to order. Clients can choose their own colours from a basic palette of 300 shades and select their own weaves, pile heights, designs and sizes.

There are two grades of knottage that can be chosen for the wool carpets, either 80 or 100 knots per square inch. The rugs can be made of Tibetan wool, silk or pashmina.

The range of designs within the Eclipse collections and the flexibility to design almost anything for specific clients, has led to a great deal of interest and success among interior designers and architects, one of whom has said that 'these are without doubt the most beautifully designed and made rugs that I have ever seen'.

Eclipse has now also launched a range of cotton dhurries made in Jaipur.

Eclipse has received varied commissions from five-star hotel chains, property developers, high-end retail outlets and, of course, countless private clients.

Contact Details

Eclipse Carpets Ltd
Luke Irwin
The Old Foundry
Tollard Royal
Wiltshire
SP5 5PS
Tel: 01725 553000 / 07766 114429
Email: luke@eclipse-carpets.com
Website: www.eclipse-carpets.com

J Brooke Fairbairn was founded over 35 years ago when Sir Brooke Fairbairn realised there was a niche in the market for a small company offering a highly personalised service with a selection of top-quality fabrics. Originating as a converter of prints, the company quickly evolved into its present form as a wholesale supplier to the retail and furnishing trade.

Sir Brooke bought and renovated the magnificent Newmarket Railway Station from where his company has operated ever since.

The company grew further when he acquired the stock and trading name of Charles Holliday in 1989, thus enlarging the customer base throughout the length and breadth of the UK and abroad. Prints, especially toiles, velvets, damasks, upholstery and plain materials make up the range, as well as a widely acclaimed and popular collection of Beatrix Potter prints.

Sir Brooke prides himself on the company's well-deserved reputation for a personal service and swift delivery of pieces or cut lengths from stock of all designs held in the Railway Station at Newmarket.

Paradiso Colour 3

J. Brooke Fairbairn & Company

Sir Brooke celebrates 55 years in the furnishing fabrics business this year, with his collections as innovative and carefully chosen as ever.

Contact Details

J. Brooke Fairbairn & Company
The Railway Station
Newmarket
Suffolk
CB8 9WT
Tel: 01638 665766
Fax: 01638 665124
Email: brookefairbairn@btconnect.com

Contact Details

Fetherstonhaugh Fabrics
The Walled Garden
Uppark
Nr Petersfield
Hampshire
GU31 5QR
Tel: 01730 825 627
Fax: 01730 826 057
Email: sophie@spa24.co.uk

Clockwise, from above left: Bed at Uppark decorated in white voile; Dressing table; Voile dressing table, Laetitia curtains; Laetitia fabric

Fetherstonhaugh Fabrics

Traditional floral country colours characterise the fabrics on offer from this company's exclusive range. Fabrics can also be custom-made to customers' requirements of colour, to ensure a complete match for a classical interior design scheme.

Having worked with two prominent London interior design houses, Sophie Meade-Fetherstonhaugh started her own fabric business in 1980. She decided to produce hand-printed designs and began selling them to interior decorators.

Although some of Sophie's designs are machine-printed, and she imports Swiss voiles, her collection of fabrics is still predominately hand-printed and can be placed on any material, although glazed chintz is a favourite.

The range is strongly traditional and mostly floral in country colours. To add variety, there is also a collection of mini prints. These are ideal for use on lampshades or for lining the curtains of four poster beds.

The two bestsellers in the collection are Laetitia and Theodora Tulip. Sophie used both of these designs for the refurbishment of Uppark after a disastrous fire.

Fired Earth

Fired Earth fabrics blend together harmoniously to create casual decorative interiors for both city homes and getaway retreats.

Inspired by natural elements and soft, earthy colours, Fired Earth fabrics include self patterned linens, velvets, chenilles, classic crewel work and fine botanical embroideries.

Every day Fired Earth's team of 40 home designers, based all over the country, are working to help interpret your ideas and inspiration so they can become a reality in your home.

Contact Details

Fired Earth
Chelsea Harbour Design Centre
North Dome G18/19
London SW10 0XE
Tel: 020 7351 7760
Fax: 020 7351 7752

Head Office:
6 Stinsford Road
Poole
Dorset BH17 0SW
Tel: 01202 266900
Fax: 01202 266901
Email: sales@gpjbaker.com
Website: www.gpjbaker.com

This trade-only company buys exclusive fabrics direct from mills in Europe, the USA and the UK, to provide the best quality fabrics at affordable prices. It offers a personal service to all its customers; this is what sets it apart from the rest.

Fitzroy Fabrics

Fitzroy Fabrics' regular stock is readily available. It can offer thousands of metres of ever-changing stock from its retail outlet based in the heart of the Cotswolds, including own ranges and designer clearance. Therefore it does not produce sample books, but instead offers a bespoke sampling service – customers just outline their schemes or project requirements. Orders are delivered swiftly to the destination of choice. The regularly updated website gives just a small taste of what is on offer.

People who own shops and would like the opportunity to offer Fitzroy Fabrics' regular stock direct to their own clients, can call to discuss the possibilities of being supplied with hangers. Fire- and stain-resistant services are available at minimal cost.

Traditional to contemporary
A wide selection of both contemporary and traditional designs is offered, including fabulous country style themed fabrics, including farmyard animals, game birds and fish, which are very popular with country sporting hotels. More traditional, sumptuous chenille fabrics and heraldic designs, perfect for dining rooms, are also available, all at down-to-earth prices. Prices start at £3.75 (plus VAT) per metre for stylish striped lining as featured in Country Living Magazine.

Contact Details

Fitzroy Fabrics
Woodgrove Farm
Fulbrook, Burford
Oxfordshire
OX18 4BH
Tel: 01993 824222
Fax: 01993 822751
Email: fabrics@fitzroyfabrics.co.uk
Website: www.fitzroyfabrics.co.uk

Anna French

This 30-year-old family-run business, famous for painterly prints and wallpaper, traditional lace and luxurious weaves, has created a unique place in the furnishing industry.

Above: Diamond Pink from the Award winning Cool Comfort; Below: Bird in the Bush based on an old block print and William flock on linen from Four Linens and a Velvet; Polka Dot wallpaper from T for Teddy; Left: Tyntesfield Silk, dark brown flock printed on gold silk taffeta from Carnation Street

Anna French was founded in 1976 by Anna and John French, from the top floor of a lace mill in Ayrshire. The company soon became well known for its Victorian cotton lace produced at the mill and then for whimsical floral prints and coordinating wallpapers. Anna's style is probably best described as painterly and, indeed, much of what has inspired her has come through that medium.

The company relocated to London; the showroom on the King's Road in Chelsea opened in 1986 and the business now includes Anna's son, Jonathan and daughter, Sasha.

Anna French currently produces bold prints on linen-based cloths, sumptuous weaves and textured wall coverings. Some cloths have been stone washed to create a soft, relaxed look. The business is committed to producing superior-quality, fabulous fabrics which are carefully created, coloured and designed at affordable prices. Most are suitable for upholstery as well as window treatments. A collection of linen weaves called 'Cool Comfort' won the Homes & Gardens Fabric Awards for Best Collection in 2004. Wallpapers coordinate with the ranges and lace remains a strong part of the company's production.

Not all the company's fabrics are based on linen however; velvet, silk, hemp, viscose and cotton are also used.

Other collections include 'Four Linens and a Velvet', in which Bird in the Bush is based on an old block print. Anna wanted to keep it looking worn and faded. 'Carnation Street' features Tyntesfield, a traditional damask produced as flocked, silk taffeta.

Anna French is also famous for children's designs. The first, 'Ready Teddy Go', was produced in 1993, and more recently, 'T for Teddy' was launched.

Contact Details

Anna French
343 Kings Road, London
SW3 5ES
Tel: 020 7351 1126
Fax: 020 7274 8913
Email: enquiries@annafrench.co.uk
Website: www.annafrench.co.uk

Fox Linton

Whether you are looking for fabrics, furniture or accessories, outstanding design is at the heart of the Fox Linton experience.

Fox Linton is the result of the collaboration between the renowned designer and 'Grande Dame of Groovy' Mary Fox Linton and Philip Cadle, founder and former managing Director of Zoffany.

Together they create collections of beautifully coloured plain and textured fabrics for both traditional and contemporary contexts, alongside furniture ranges and accessories. Fox Linton also works closely with and represents Jim Thompson and features other carefully selected designer fabrics ranges that reflect the essential values of Fox Linton.

Mary's Groovy Grand signature is evidenced by such high profile projects as the award winning hotels One Aldwych in London, Carlisle Bay in Antigua and the Grove in Hertfordshire. Mary has been honoured on both sides of the Atlantic with lifetime achievement awards from The Royal Oak Foundation in New York and House and Garden.

Below: Fox Linton Bar, hand-sculpted in bronze and brass. Soft Breeze Counter chairs by John Hutton; Opposite, from top: Fox Linton Demi Lune sofa with D'Alliance Club chairs by John Hutton. Escape fabric on the windows by Jim Thompson; Fox Linton Wave fabric – a 100 per cent kid mohair, shows the impeccable palette of the Fox Linton range

Fox Linton's purpose is to provide fabrics, furniture and accessories to top interior designers and specifiers for their residential and contract projects. These have included, amongst others: The Old Vic; The Hurlingham Club; The Dorchester; The Athenaeum; The All England Tennis Club at Wimbledon; and even the provision of textiles for the costumes for ongoing productions at the Royal Opera House Covent Garden and the Harry Potter films.

Fox Linton's values lie in its impeccable design and palette, technical experience through its in-house design and technology studio, and high-quality production values for all the ranges.

Knowledgeable service is delivered through the Fox Linton showroom at Chelsea Harbour, an expansive, fresh and welcoming space in which to view the treasured collection of fabric, furniture and accessories.

Contact Details

Fox Linton
Showroom
2nd Floor, North Dome
Chelsea Harbour Design Centre
Lots Road
London SW10 0XE
Tel: 020 7368 7700
Fax: 020 7368 7701
Email: info@foxlinton.com
Website: www.foxlinton.com

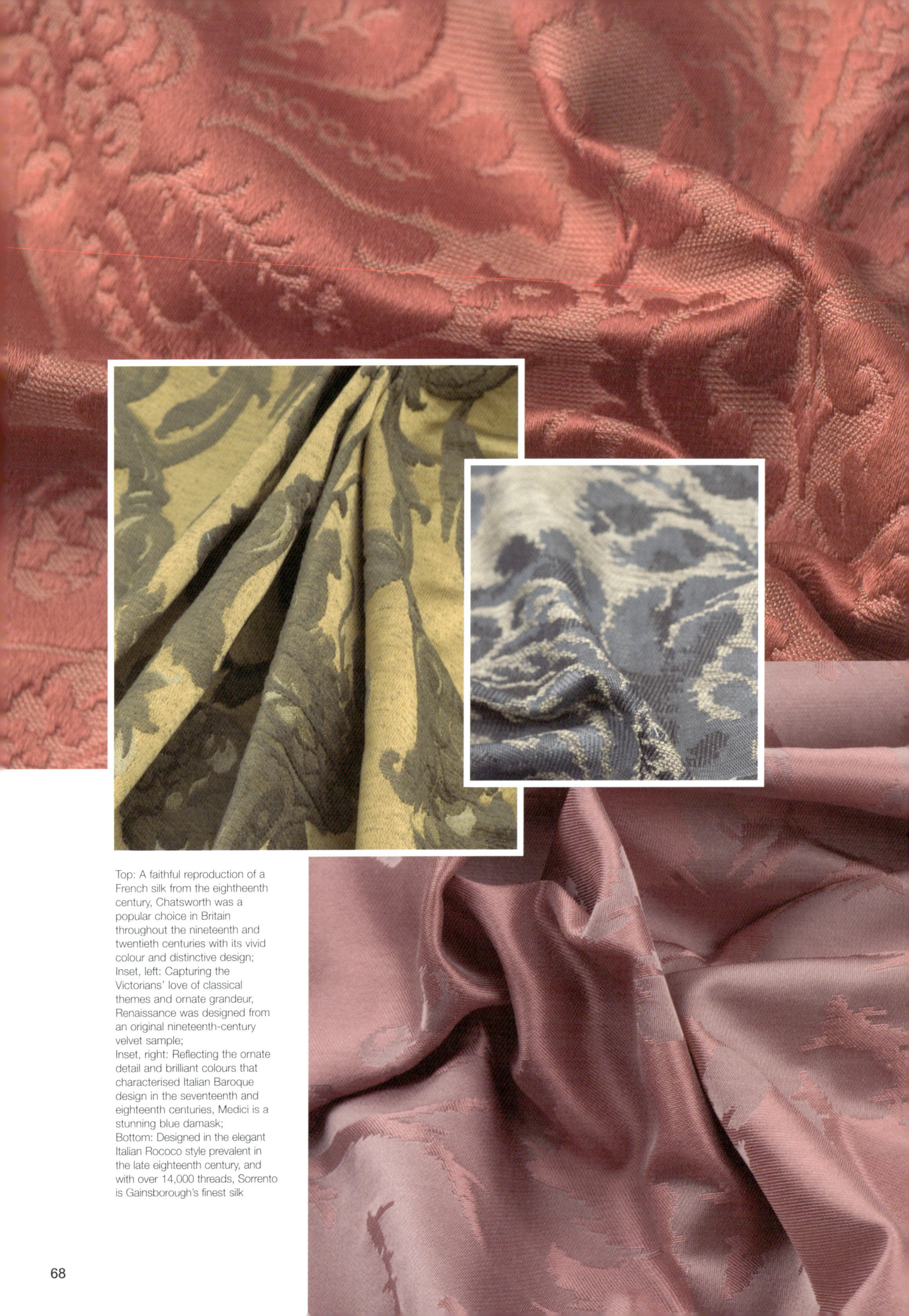

Top: A faithful reproduction of a French silk from the eightheenth century, Chatsworth was a popular choice in Britain throughout the nineteenth and twentieth centuries with its vivid colour and distinctive design;
Inset, left: Capturing the Victorians' love of classical themes and ornate grandeur, Renaissance was designed from an original nineteenth-century velvet sample;
Inset, right: Reflecting the ornate detail and brilliant colours that characterised Italian Baroque design in the seventeenth and eighteenth centuries, Medici is a stunning blue damask;
Bottom: Designed in the elegant Italian Rococo style prevalent in the late eighteenth century, and with over 14,000 threads, Sorrento is Gainsborough's finest silk

The Gainsborough Silk Weaving Company

Designers and weavers of the finest silks, damasks, brocatelle and taffetas since 1903, this is a truly unique fabric house. Tucked away in Suffolk, the old mill houses one of Britain's largest textile archives and the capability to reproduce any design in any colour using traditional techniques, with breathtaking results.

Founded by a master weaver with a passion for historical fabric and a commitment to quality, The Gainsborough Silk Weaving Company has remained true to its roots. A visit to the custom-built mill is like stepping back in time, the oak frames and ironwork mechanisms of the 1920s looms inspire a Victorian feel. Threads from countless bobbins feed through the air to be expertly wound onto a large wooden spool, whilst elsewhere, yarn is being prepared with traditional dyes in readiness for the next commission. The craftsmanship and time invested in every length of cloth is remarkable.

Testament to the quality of the fabric, Gainsborough boasts an enviable client list that includes 10 Downing Street, The Houses of Parliament and The Tate and National Galleries. In 1980, Gainsborough became a proud holder of the Royal Warrant with commissions for Buckingham Palace, Sandringham, Clarence House, Windsor Castle and Balmoral. In all these great houses, fabrics dating as far back as the fifteenth century hang resplendently, taken from Gainsborough's unique archive of over 2000 designs.

The resources and flexibility required to offer such an extensive traditional portfolio are considerable, and ironically, they are the key to the company's success today. By controlling every aspect of manufacture, Gainsborough can offer unlimited scope for customisation. Such is the company's reputation that customers frequently present a fragment of fabric from which identical metres can be woven. Furthermore, Gainsborough is happy to undertake custom weaves from as little as 20m. Whether you need an existing design colour matched to suit an intended scheme or want a completely new design created, skilled craftsmen will undertake the project at no extra cost and with no restriction on choice of yarn, drawing on a century of expertise to deliver unparalleled quality.

Contact Details

The Gainsborough Silk Weaving Company Ltd
Alexandra Road
Sudbury
Suffolk
CO10 2XH
Tel: 01787 372081
Email: sales@gainsborough.co.uk
Website: www.gainsborough.co.uk

Garin is the oldest Spanish weaver and editor still active in Spain. Founded in 1820, the company sells its products to over 30 countries.

Garin 1820

Having emerged as part of the silk weaving industry in Valencia, this family business still keeps 12 manual looms dating back to the nineteenth century, when these wonderful silk brocades were woven by hand.

Garin also weaves for other editors and produces commissioned fabrics for large contract projects.

Today, Garin is one of the very few editors that has its own factory. This allows the company to cut out the middleman and offer both incredible value for money and outstanding service.

The collections encompass hand-woven silk damasks as well as machine-woven furnishing fabrics, such as traditional damasks, chenilles and textured plains. Garin also manufactures chenille rugs, throws and tapestries.

Most collections combine one or two large repeat designs with coordinating plains and small designs, and 95 per cent are of quality suitable for upholstery use.

Contact Details

Garin 1820 SA
Alfredo Martinez
C/Quart 45 - 46113 Moncada
Valencia, Spain
Tel: +34 961 309023
Fax: +34 961 395864
Email: garin@garin1820.com

London showroom
Brian Lawrence/Oliver Kratz
Unit 2/9 South Dome, 2nd Floor
Chelsea Harbour Design Centre
London SW10 0XE
Tel: 020 7351 6496
Freephone: 0800 3897754
Fax: 020 7351 3761
Email: chelsea@garin1820.com

Left and right: Samarkanda Collection
Centre: Mogambo Collection

Hamilton Weston

This small company specialises in the reproduction and recreation of classic wallpapers. These wallpapers can be recreated from originals held in-house or from originals provided by the client.

Robert Weston carefully redraws designs, either from Hamilton Weston's extensive collection of period originals, or from document fragments supplied for restoration projects. Designs currently in production date from 1690-1960. Some are available as machine prints; others are hand-printed and may therefore be coloured to order. This gives clients extra flexibility as colours can be adjusted to fit in with each particular scheme. Often, varying the colour can make a period design look very contemporary. A selection of wallpaper borders is also available.

Clients' designs may be reproduced where there is enough of the original available for a pattern match. Bespoke designs can also be created in true period style (see the Imperial Bee illustration).

As well as producing custom designs and recreating documentary patterns, the company's extensive archive may be of interest to clients looking for something unique. Wallpapers are regularly supplied for film and TV productions. The showroom offers a comprehensive selection of interesting and unusual wallpapers from original sources.

Retail prices range from £32-£190 inclusive of VAT per 10m roll.

The company is European agent for Adelphi Paperhangings Incorporated, which makes exquisite hand block wallpapers using traditional techniques and natural cotton paper. The designs are reproduced from eighteenth-century and early nineteenth-century documents. These papers are custom-printed to order, with a minimum of just three rolls. Adelphi hand block prints range from £188-£620 inclusive of VAT per 10m roll.

Contact Details

Hamilton Weston Wallpapers Ltd
(Trade and Retail)
18 St. Mary's Grove
Richmond
Surrey
TW9 1UY
Tel: 020 8940 4850
Fax: 020 8332 0296
Website: www.hamiltonweston.com

Hand-printed wallpapers by Hamilton Weston. Clockwise from top left: Imperial Bee (created in 2004 in Napoleonic style); Carlyle Damask c.1828; Twickenham c.1750; On the edge c.1960; Royal Crescent c.1775; Fynedon Gothik c.1790; Holdenby Peacock c.1890; Edwardian Damask c.1901

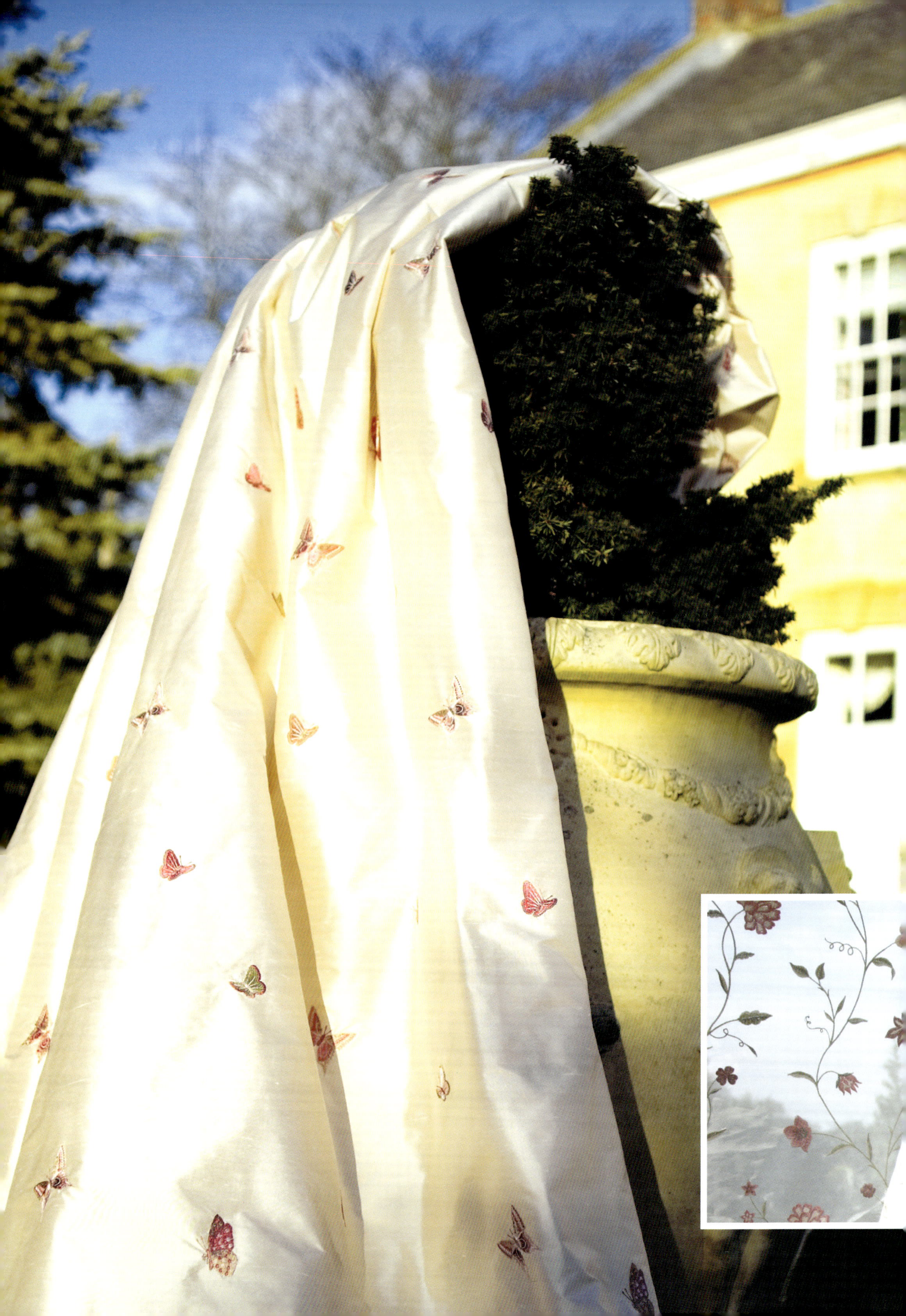

For generations, Hare of England has been supplying quality suiting and tweed. More recently, the company took a new direction and now specialises purely in silks from around the world.

James Hare Silks

Established in 1865, James Hare Ltd was originally a merchant and distributor of woollens and worsted fabrics to the tailoring trade. James Hare, the founder, had an excellent eye for both quality and value, realising from the beginning that the chief factor of success was good customer relations and high standards. These principles have been the foundations of the business and have been passed down to the current generation.

For many decades Hare of England's brand was well known throughout the world for high-quality suiting and tweeds. In 1983, the changing business climate created new challenges for the family and it was decided that an alternative direction was required; James Hare Silks was born. It now supplies silks from around the world and is one of the largest distributors in Europe. Traditionally renowned for its huge plain range, the company now offers an ever-expanding number of eye-catching embroideries.

Designing new collections is paramount to the company's success. An integral part of the design process is ensuring that ranges are not only attractive but also practical and usable. James Hare Silks' unique sense of style and colour ensure that the company maintains its well-deserved reputation for beautiful fabrics.

The company turned its attention to soft furnishings in 2004 with silk cushion covers. These complement the existing fabrics, ensuring that interior design is easier for its clients. Building on its initial success, James Hare Silks has continued to expand this fast-growing collection.

Today James Hare Silks enjoys a long-standing reputation for service, quality and creativity. This ensures that the company remains a market leader in silk design and distribution.

Prices range from £15 to £70 per metre.

Opposite: Butterfly Embroidered Dupion; Below, from left: Floral Embroidered Voile; Regal Dupion; Above, from top: Shot Taffeta; Printed Matka

Contact Details

James Hare Silks
PO Box 72
Monarch House
Queen Street
Leeds
LS1 ILX
Tel: 01132 431 204
Fax: 01132 347 648
Email: sales@jamesharesilks.co.uk
Website: www.jamesharesilks.co.uk

The Percy Bass Decorator's Guide

From top: Chalvington, a late eighteenth-century French design; Carinthia, a mid nineteenth-century French design; Caterina, a mid to late eighteenth-century French design; Toile d'Albert, an early nineteenth-century French design with matching wallpaper

Nicholas Herbert Ltd.

Founded in 1989, Nicholas Herbert Ltd. moved to its present showroom in the Lots Road, Chelsea in 1993. The company specialises in the reproduction of antique or 'document' textile designs for both fabrics and wallpapers.

These antique documents are sourced worldwide from a network of markets and dealers. They are predominately French in origin. Once the company has selected a document to reproduce, it is sent to the mill in France, to be re-engraved to fit onto a suitable new fabric or base cloth. As the original pieces were almost always designed to fit onto tables or machines of approximately 90cm width, there is always a bit of pulling and tugging to enlarge or reduce them to fit onto contemporary fabric widths, which are more in the line of 130cm to 145cm.

A few screens are always added to the design, allowing the use of more colours to achieve the delicately faded look of an eighteenth-century original. Where, for instance, an original flower may have been one shade of red, it will have been washed so often that the piece that is bought will appear to have faded into perhaps three shades. This is what the company aims to reproduce.

Perfect colour match
The next step is the re-colouring of the design. With eighteenth-century designs in particular, the original colourway of the document works best. Therefore an eighteenth-century colourway is always found in all productions.

The colouring is done entirely in-house with Nick Herbert and Nicky Bailey bickering merrily away about the merits of their respective watercolour 'brush outs'. Once a truce is declared the brush outs are sent to France to be converted into hand trials on cloth.

Hand trials fly backwards and forwards across the Channel until the desired look is achieved. The whole process from sending a document to the mill and the engraver to receiving the 'stock' usually takes about a year and costs an absolute fortune. However, Nicholas Herbert thinks it is worth both the time and the money to produce designs that are both authentic and beautiful.

Prices for wallpapers range from £42 to £65 per roll. Fabrics range from £45 to £90 per metre.

Contact Details

Nicholas Herbert Ltd.
118 Lots Road
London
SW10 0RJ
Tel: 020 7376 5596
Fax: 020 7376 5572
Email: enquiries@nicholasherbert.com
Website: www.nicholasherbert.com

From left: Traditional Passementerie; Contemporary Trimmings; Frog, Tassel Fringe & Beads

Manufacturing for trade-only clients, Heritage Trimmings has a trade brochure that includes a fixed pricing structure and is available at no cost upon request. This simple to use and understandable brochure has a comprehensive listing of the most popular designs, making design choices and quoting for a scheme much easier. However, the company's bespoke design service offers you the opportunity to create a completely original look.

Heritage has an extensive and impressive portfolio of trimmings, which contains contemporary, traditional and historic samples. To view this, contact the design team, who will arrange a convenient time to visit you at your showroom. Clients are always encouraged to visit the team at their factory, which is a fascinating facility.

The bespoke service is easy to use. Simply send cuttings of your chosen fabrics, indicating what styles of trimmings you need, and by return you will receive colour matchings (in the exact materials your trimmings will be made of) for you to choose from. The design team will help you with colouring, ensure the trimming achieves a balanced look, and offer advice on style choice.

Heritage Trimmings stands for service and quality. Place an order with the company in complete confidence that your passementerie will be made to the highest standards by dedicated experienced staff at the Derby factory, and you can expect delivery on time.

Heritage Trimmings

From a simple button tuft to the completion of a major project, this company's customers can rely on high-quality bespoke trimmings for that perfect finish. On offer are not just tassels, ropes and fringes, but 'jewellery of the house'.

Contact Details

Heritage Trimmings Ltd
The Old Mess Room
Colombo Street
Derby, DE23 8LW
Tel: 01332 343953
Fax: 01332 298443
Email: email@heritagetrimmings.co.uk
Website: www.heritagetrimmings.co.uk

Allegra Hicks

Allegra Hicks, the internationally acclaimed lifestyle designer, has created a beautiful emporium at her London flagship store where she showcases her award-winning textile, wallpaper and rug collections.

Colour, pattern and texture form the basic vocabulary of Allegra's distinctive design language. The results translate into original, stylish and elegant homes, which she creates together with her husband, Ashley Hicks, the accomplished furniture and interior designer. Her style successfully marries old and new for an eclectic look.

Allegra's fabric collection features her classic India-inspired cotton prints, including the ever-popular Tree of Life design. Her linen collection includes larger, bolder one-colour prints, such as her signature pattern, Fans, on neutral-coloured textured linens. The silk collection comes in an array of stunning colours, with patterns such as the stylish Desert Flower delicately woven into the fabric. New to the market is a collection of cut velvets in geometric patterns, which tie in beautifully with her prints and wallpapers.

The Allegra Hicks wallpaper collection works with almost any decorating style and ranges from a more subtle two-tone colour palette to sophisticated metallics, depending on the desired effect. Patterns also come in a useful selection of scales.

To tie the room together in a clever and effective way, clients can choose from a selection of beautiful hand-stitched, flat-weave rugs or have a bespoke rug designed in one of her many famous designs. Her rug collection includes a variety of qualities ranging from dhurries and kilims to wool and silk hand-knotted rugs, all creating a warm and comfortable centrepiece to the living space.

Fabric prices range from £56 to £108 per metre. Wallpaper is priced at £45 per roll. Rug prices range from £215 to £675 per square metre.

Contact Details

Allegra Hicks Ltd
28 Cadogan Place
London SW1X 9RX
Tel: 020 7235 3322
Fax: 020 7235 3325
Email: interiors@allegrahicks.com

Hodsoll McKenzie was formed in the late 1980s, when Mark Butcher and Alex McKenzie worked together to design bespoke fabrics for the Mark Hotel in New York, one of the first boutique hotels.

They wanted to create a look that was classic and reminiscent of an English country house, but which was understated, informal and timeless.

The first designs had lived-in qualities that helped coin the phrase Shabby Chic. Some of these still grace the collection today. In May 2005, Hodsoll McKenzie was acquired by Zimmer + Rohde, as a fourth label to the company.

As a permanent part of the Zimmer + Rohde group, Hodsoll McKenzie continues to develop and advance the collection, constantly moving forward with new innovative designs and fresh colouring.

Hodsoll McKenzie marries classic ideas with modern living.

From top: Chrysanthamum & Berry, 20924-502; Ladies & Gentlemen, 20920-505; Bramble Leaf, 20005-411

Creating a look that is both classic and timeless, while retaining a contemporary feel with distinctly British characteristics, this collection is constantly evolving and pushing forward with inventive ideas.

Hodsoll McKenzie

Contact Details

Hodsoll McKenzie
15 Chelsea Harbour Design Centre
Lots Road
London
SW10 0XE
Tel: 020 7351 7115
Fax: 020 7351 5661
Email: info.uk@zimmer-rohde.com
Website: www.zimmer-rohde.com

Top, from left: The finest wool sateen, superb lustre, drapes and upholsters well, available in 32 colours and can be dyed to meet colour specifications; Colours in harmony, beautifully coloured multi stripes in favourite wool sateen quality, available in eight shades; Cashmere wool, soft to the hand, these warm autumnal colours bring out the quality of natural fibres, available in 21 patterns; Middle, from left: Ever popular robust corduroy, quality woven in traditional and fancy colours, 100 per cent cotton; Mohair velvet, the comfort of natural fibres, woven to perfection in 16 shades, 100 per cent mohair pile; Hacienda linens, quality 100 per cent linen in five different qualities, on natural tones to match the natural fibre; Bottom, from left: Loch Lomond Cashmere, soft to the touch, 100 per cent pure cashmere for 100 per cent pure luxury; Chenille, 19 colours ranging from natural to bright shades to suit every style, in viscose, cotton and polyester; Kelly Hoppen perfect neutral collection cashmere – the highlight is 16 pure cashmere materials in plain, checks and stripes, inspired by Holland & Sherry's Savile Row heritage

Holland & Sherry

Inspirational is the best way to describe this interior collection, launched specifically for the home.

For some years, the top interior designers in Western Europe and the USA have looked to the clothing world for inspirational new fabrics and ideas. Woollens, tweeds, silks and linens are becoming important components of the smartest and most elegant homes. Holland & Sherry, cloth weavers, merchants and suppliers of luxury textiles to the fashion industry since 1836, have responded to this demand and launched a collection specifically for the home. The Holland & Sherry interior collection offers endless possibilities, from pinstriped cloth upholstered on a wall, textured silks on chairs, natural linens draped as curtains, fine wool covering a sofa, or simply a cashmere throw to add the finishing touches.

Inspired by Savile Row Heritage

Holland & Sherry worked closely with Kelly Hoppen to create an exquisite collection. The result is a beautiful range in Kelly's Perfect Neutrals colour palette of natural tones and textures.

For the future, Holland & Sherry have exciting plans to launch an exclusive print and embroidery collection. Other new additions include a range of vibrant colours and designs in woven linens.

Kelly Hoppen's Perfect Neutrals collection: Linens, cottons, boiled wools, parachute (a brilliant fabric which Kelly often uses for curtains) plain and embroidered lustre and faux suede

Contact Details

Holland & Sherry Ltd
9/10 Savile Row
London W1S 3PF
England
Tel: 020 7437 0404
Fax: 020 7734 6110
Email: enquiries@hollandandsherry.co.uk

Below: Richard Humphries' latest weaves using archive designs. From left: Leicester Silk and Cotton; Eisenhower Taffeta Silk; St Paul Silk; Cotton

Humphries Weaving Company

If your historic mansion needs to be refurbished with reproductions of eighteenth-century silk designs, you are likely to find yourself speaking to the Humphries Weaving Company.

From top: Weaving by hand in the design studio; Colour trials being woven prior to production; Custom-dyed yarns for a period restoration

The silk weaving industry took root in the UK relatively late, founded in the sixteenth century for the making of ribbons and trims – the so-called narrow branch of silk weaving. The influx of Huguenots into England in 1685 following the revocation of the Edict of Nantes gave a great boost to English silk weaving. The industry was originally based around Spitalfields, Bow and Bethnal Green in London, and among the weaving families were many Huguenots. In the early nineteenth century, some moved away from London to avoid the city's tax on weavers, and settled in towns such as Braintree, Halstead and Sudbury on the Essex and Suffolk border.

In 1966, the 15-year-old Richard Humphries began his design apprenticeship with Warners, the UK's leading silk weaving company at that time. Based in Braintree, the company had 85 hand looms and 60 power looms, but believing that manmade fibres would soon completely replace silk, it had only three hand weavers.

Five years later, the entire weaving department closed down, threatening the future of silk weaving in the UK. However, just as Warner was closing its doors in Braintree, Humphries was beginning his own weaving operation in nearby Sudbury, making furnishing silks.

The young Humphries raised what capital he could and managed to save hand looms, some Jacquard cards and the Jacquard card-punching machine to create new designs. Sadly, the remaining looms and 3000 sets of Jacquard cards were subsequently destroyed.

With nowhere to set up his equipment, Humphries faced an uncertain future. Eventually, premises were found and he installed his looms and equipment, creating custom window blinds and textured furnishings.

From these small beginnings the business flourished, and in 1975 Humphries moved to Devere Mill in Castle Hedingham in Essex. This allowed him to reinstate Jacquard looms, and one of the firm's early orders was for the refurbishment of the King's Apartments at Hampton Court Palace. In 1990, looms were reinstalled in the restored Warners New Mills at Braintree, and silk throwstering and yarn dyeing were soon well established at Castle Hedingham.

However, in 2000, Humphries considered modernising the company's manufacturing processes, and it began weaving its unique silks on automatic looms. Having returned to Sudbury in 2004 and employed modern weaving techniques at the new Sudbury Silk Mills premises, Humphries Weaving is now equipped to custom-weave figured textiles in silk and many other sumptuous fabrics. These can be seen in the Humphries display at Alton Brooke Ltd in the Chelsea Harbour Design Centre.

Contact Details

Humphries
c/o Alton-Brooke
2–25 Chelsea Harbour Design Centre
Lots Road, London SW10 0XE
Tel: 020 7376 7008
Fax: 020 7376 7009
Email: info@alton-brooke.co.uk
Website: www.alton-brooke.co.uk

The Percy Bass Decorator's Guide

Left: Rug, Maracaibo; Below right: Vernon Panton Rocking Chair upholstered in fabric Arlequin, Rug Maracaibo, Sheer floral fabric Guyana; Bottom: Fabric Vevey

A passion for furniture and commitment to offer the best in cutting-edge design for the interior is key to Interdesign's approach. On offer is a wide collection of contemporary furniture, lighting, fabric, rugs and soft accessories by the finest Italian brands.

For inspiration, the showroom in Chelsea Harbour's Design Centre is an invaluable stop. The furniture is mostly Italian, including many well-known brands, but individuality comes by sourcing from smaller manufacturers with an eye for innovative design. The approach is diverse and new products arrive on a weekly basis providing a refreshing environment for all visitors.

Trends change, but furniture and home accessories that are carefully planned and skilfully produced is what good design is about; furniture that is beautiful yet fulfils its purpose. This is a key requirement of all products. Furthermore, as urban living often means a smaller living space, practical interiors are required and key pieces can provide a range of applications.

Exclusively on display is the Missoni Home collection of fabrics, rugs, candles, throws, cushions, bed linens and table accessories produced with innovative attention to colour, in an array of patterned stripes, checks, zigzags or graduation.

Prices for fabrics range from £48 per metre to £154 per metre. Rugs range from £324 to £6000 and soft accessories from £8 to £760.

Contact Details

Interdesign UK
G30 Chelsea Harbour Design Centre
London
SW10 OXE
Tel: 020 7376 5272
Fax: 020 7376 3020
Email: info@interdesignuk.com

Interdesign UK

Featuring innovative designs with a sense of individuality, this constantly updated range of furniture has a distinctly Italian feel. It is complemented by a home collection of fabrics, rugs and table accessories.

Contact Details

Kathryn Ireland
Fairbank Studios
65–69 Lots Road
London SW10 0RN
Tel: 020 7751 4554
Fax: 020 7751 4555
Website: www.kathrynireland.com

Kathryn Ireland's designs are hand-printed onto natural hemp, giving a soft and slightly antiqued effect, while the colourways, bright primaries, lavender, sage and earth tones, lend a fresh, vital look to the range.

Kathryn's whimsical Quilt Collection was inspired by nineteenth-century French quilting fabrics and includes paisleys, florals and tickings. The Toile Collection includes a modern toile and large florals, complemented by bold stripes and checks. Taking inspiration from traditional Indonesian island prints, the Batik Collection combines vibrant colours with the lines effect of the ancient art of hot cracked wax designs. A visit to India inspired the scrolls and simple prints of the Indian Collection. In addition to the prints, there is also a Woven Linen Collection, which includes sheers, basketweave linen and woven linen stripes, as well as rich linen plaids, damask and Jacquards.

The showroom is located close to Chelsea Harbour Design Centre, and represents several Californian fabric design companies.

Kathryn Ireland

Vintage textile designs from around the world are reworked to stunning effect in this sumptuous range of fabrics. Kathryn is an English interior designer who lives and works in California and France, and these influences show in her collections.

For over 200 years this company has specialised in the design and production of classic tartans, plaids, paisleys, sheers, damasks and plains, all woven at its mill in the highlands of Scotland. And it has been in family ownership for all this time.

The Isle Mill

The Isle Mill, a division of Macnaughton Holdings Ltd, specialises in wool and wool mixture fabrics and has Jacquard and Dobby capability, both available in piece- and yarn-dyed qualities. The resulting fabrics are versatile, practical and can be used for a variety of interior applications. Most are suitable for contract as well as domestic interiors, as the fabrics are hardwearing and inherently flame-retardant. Over 2000 stock fabrics are available for selection from pattern books stocked by selected interior designers and retail soft furnishing

Opposite, anticlockwise from top: Turnberry Sofa in Lomond Stripe Champagne – 100 per cent wool; Fabric out of the Lochwinnoch range; Shetland Throws – 97 per cent wool; Left: Wing Chair in Jura Sky (Hebrides range) – 100 per cent wool; Right: Lift Top Storage Stool in Kettla Check Oatmeal; Below: Fabric, Sienna Inchinnan out of the Lochwinnoch range – 100 per cent wool

Contact Details

The Isle Mill
Tower House
Ruthvenfield Road
Perth
Scotland
PH1 3UN
Tel: 01738 609090
Fax: 01738 604010
Email: islemill@macnaughton-group.com
Website: www.islemill.com

London Showroom:
c/o Borderline, Unit 12, 3rd Floor
Chelsea Harbour Design Centre
London SW10 0XE
Tel: 020 7823 3567
Fax: 020 7351 7644

showrooms. Retail prices range between £38 and £55 per metre.

The Isle Mill prides itself on its flexibility and is accordingly happy to undertake bespoke design projects tailor-made to individual specifications. As well as products sold under its own name, the company also produces products for leading wholesale fabric houses in Europe and USA.

The UK and European distribution for Thomas Dare was acquired by Macnaughton Holdings Ltd in September 2003 and the sales, design, administration and warehousing functions of Thomas Dare are now based at the group's purpose-built premises in Perth, Scotland. The brand specialises in hand-woven cotton and silk fabrics, retailing at prices between £16 and £65 per metre.

Bespoke furniture

The Isle Mill launched its first collection of bespoke upholstered furniture in 2005. Carefully chosen to complement the company's high-quality woven fabric, each model has been designed and manufactured in the UK to the highest specification. The stylish range comprises three sofa shapes, all in five sizes, together with loveseats and armchairs. There is also a separate tub chair and wing chair accessorised by two shapes of lift top storage stools.

Under a new brand licensing agreement, Viyella Home fabrics are being designed and manufactured by the group and will be presented to the market soon.

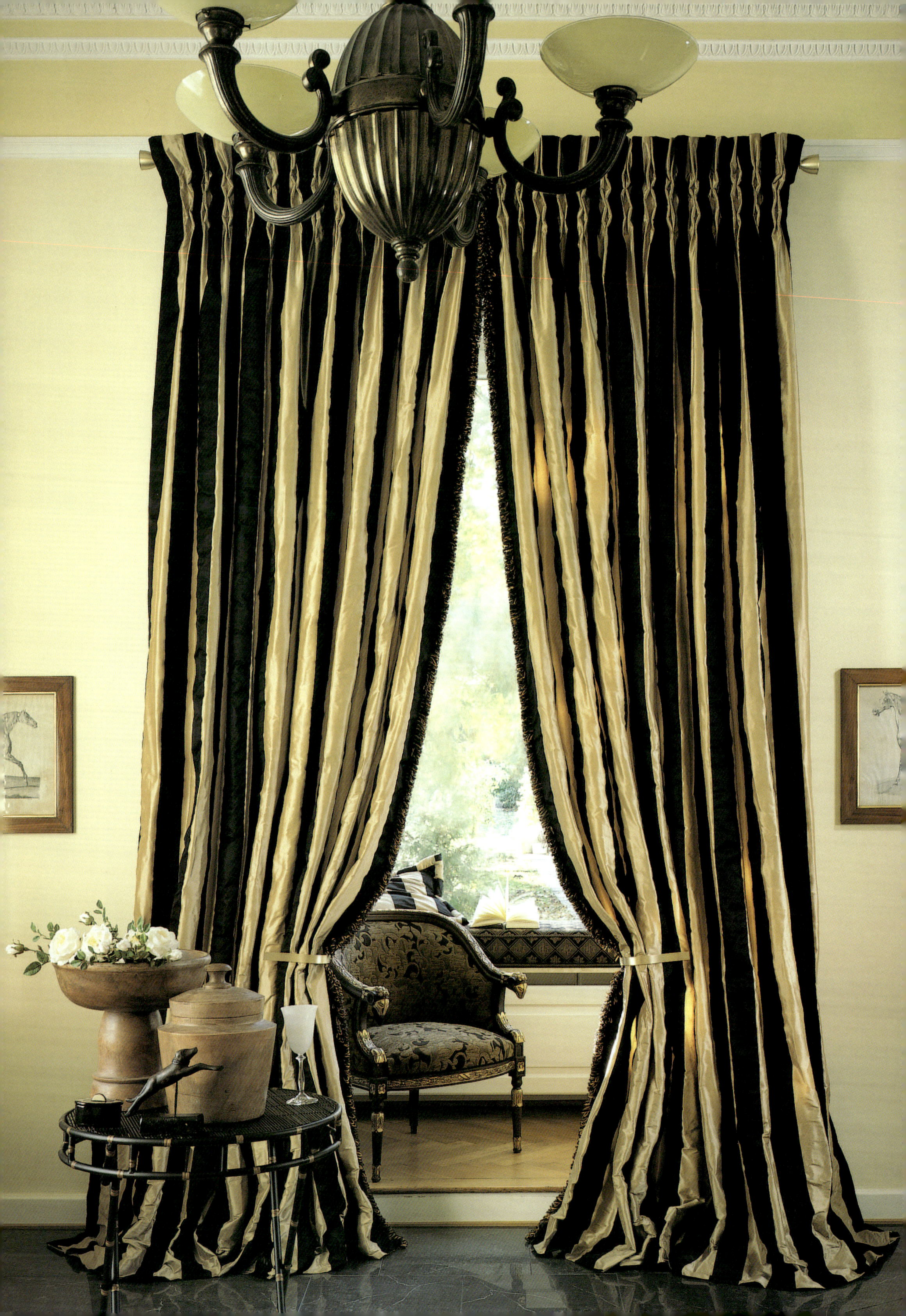

Jab was founded in 1946 by Josef Anstoetz in Bielefeld, Germany and is one of the world's leading fabric and carpet editors. It is still a family business run by brothers Ralph, Stephan and Claus Anstoetz. The company launches fabric collections in its Dream Living range twice a year for worldwide distribution.

From beautiful silks and silk damasks (there are also damasks in a linen/cotton mix) to faux suede, everything in the range is available in a variety of colours. To complete a window treatment, voiles are made to complement collections and can be in colourful patterns or embroidered. Another addition to the Jab interior is a range of custom-made carpets and rugs that can be coordinated into a scheme.

Jab has been in the UK for 25 years, and its furnishing and curtain fabrics have been used to decorate contemporary homes, boats, hotels and palaces, as well as serving the contract market. Luxury hotels with Jab soft furnishing fabrics include the Palais Coburg in Vienna and the Mirador Kempinski on Lake Geneva.

To complete the Jab interior, custom-made carpets and rugs can be coordinated into a scheme, and for a younger, more colourful home, subsidiary company Club Creation Niemann fills the gap. Other subsidiaries include Chivasso, with its strong, vibrant colours, and Carlucci, an elegant, exclusively themed range.

And if a designer also needs a making up service, curtains, cushions, bedspreads and quilting can all be made in the Jab workshops, an additional service from this unique fabric company.

Contact Details

Jab International Furnishings Ltd
1/15–16 Chelsea Harbour Design Centre
London
SW10 0XE
Tel: 020 7349 9323
Fax: 020 7349 9282
Website: www.jab.de

Jab International Furnishings Ltd

This family-run business, established in Germany, now operating out of London, and with 3000 fabrics in 20,000 colourways all from stock, is a one-stop resource for interior decorators. Whether it is plains, coordinated patterns or beautiful silk collections, this company specialises in strong, vibrant colours and lifestyle coordinates. If a designer is looking for an exact shade of silk taffeta to complete a room design, they need look no further.

Opposite: Villaverde 1-2482-121, Salinero 1-2483-129, Jalta 1-7671-199, Baron 1-9096-197, decorative track system, Amphore 5-7663-620; Right, from top: Excelsa-Rose 1-7318-171, Pisano 1-6313-520, Sikkim 1-7215-245, Emporio 1-7495-110; Fauna, 5918/990 170x240cm, design by Bernd Benninghoff, hand-tufted and hand-designed with a sculpting tool; Lovely 1-2429-148, Moondrops 1-2425-146

The name Kenzo conjures up images of freedom, diversity and bright vibrant colours. The founder created an unsuspected alchemy of different cultures, East and West, which have found expression in amazing associations of colours, materials and prints.

Fusion of fashion and art
Since 2003, Antonio Marras has been entrusted with the artistic direction of the Kenzo collections. In addition to the fashion collections this also finds expression in Kenzo Maison, which is sold through Lelievre. Naturally akin to the spirit of Kenzo, he has developed a rich, poetic world made of a diversity of influences and a fusion between fashion and other forms of art.

Inspired by craftsmanship, symbolic and cultural objects, Antonio Marras invents a contemporary language and creates designs that tell stories for people who love freedom, authenticity and originality. The contrast between his unbridled intellectual nomadism and a strong grounding in everyday life is in perfect synergy with the Kenzo state of mind.

'What I admire in Kenzo is its modernity and the personal way of mixing seemingly different genres and styles and the natural poetry that happens when they are assembled. Designing for Kenzo is a very strong emotion, a real challenge', explains Marras.

The Kenzo Maison collection includes fabrics, cushions, ready-made curtains, lamps and many other home accessories. A selection can be viewed at the Lelievre showrooms in the Rue du Mail, Paris and in the Chelsea Harbour Design Centre in London.

Contact Details

Kenzo Maison
distributed by Lelievre (UK) Ltd
108–110 Chelsea Harbour Design Centre
London
SW10 OXE
Tel: 020 7352 4798
Fax: 020 7352 9569
Email: enquiries@lelievre.tm.fr
Website: www.lelievre.tm.fr

Kenzo Maison

Colourful, vibrant, geometric, cutting-edge and contemporary, this collection of weaves, prints, velvets and voiles embodies the natural poetry and creative freedom of Antonio Marras.

Robert Kime

This decorating business specialises in high-quality fabrics and wallpapers inspired by a range of aesthetic traditions, as well as light fittings and custom-made furniture.

The interior designer Robert Kime is known for his exquisite taste in decorating classically elegant rooms using his own fabric and wallpaper collections. His decorating business is run from Wiltshire. Fabrics, predominately printed on couture linen, include a collection of Arts & Crafts designs in the manner of Morris and Voysey, an Uzbek- and Mogul-inspired collection in exquisite colours and a traditional country house collection of muted designs. The fabrics have an ageless look and help to create timeless rooms with great character.

For decorators looking for inspiration and superb quality, there is the silk printed Tashkent, a fabric created from an eighteenth-century panel, and a new collection called Kandelli, inspired by Turkish hand-blocked prints in various colourations. There is also a range of woven and Ottoman silks.

Rooms created around clients' antique furniture are also enhanced by Robert Kime's collection of light fittings and custom furniture. These are faithful replicas of selected antique originals and are made locally. All of the fabrics are British-made, but there are some Turkish cushions and throws in vibrant colours for those seeking refreshingly different accessories.

Contact Details

Robert Kime
121 Kensington Church Street
London W8 7LP
Tel: 020 7229 0886
Fax: 020 7229 0766
Email: london@robertkime.com
Website: www.robertkime.com

Top Left: Marmara Linen from the Kandelli Collection;
Top Right: Coat and Hat Stand;
Bottom Left: Green Floral Damask;
Bottom Right: Embroidered cushions and throws with a Bannerman Lamp

The Percy Bass Decorator's Guide

Contact Details

Krams Ugo Ltd
Deans Drive
Edgware
Middlesex
HA8 9NU
Tel: 020 8906 8656
Fax: 020 8906 8822
Email: enquiries@kramsugo.co.uk

With its in-house curtain-making workroom, this company stocks one of the largest ranges of voiles in the UK and has a list of prestigious clients including luxury hotels. Other products include sheers, muslins and flame-retardant designs.

Krams Ugo

With over 30,000 metres in stock, Krams Ugo offers from its brand, KU Excellence, one of the largest ranges of voiles in the UK, with sizes from 120cm to 420cm. The company also stocks numerous sheers and muslins up to 300cm and a comprehensive range of flame-retardant designs.

Curtain call
Having been established for over 40 years, the in-house, trade-only, voile curtain-making workroom supplies contract furnishers for some of the world's finest hotels. Clients include interior designers at some of the most prestigious addresses and at retail furnishers throughout the UK.

Fabrics can also be custom-made to suit the specific needs of the client.

Over the last ten years Brian Lawrence has developed his own label collections of fabrics, which have expanded to include complementary wallpaper and bone china.

The Authentic Crewels Collection comprises over 18 designs specially created by Brian Lawrence in a UK colour palette, from muted cream on cream to strong but cool blues on cream and vibrant multis. Some designs include a silk or gold wire outline option for a richer, more opulent finish. Traditionally made pure Kashmir wool is hand-sewn onto loomed cotton to create variety and depth of texture, making a stunning splash as drapes and bedspreads, high note cushion covers, wall hangings, or light upholstery. Prices start from around £34 per metre.

The Ribbons & Toile Collection is based on classic French and English elements. Printed on natural cream 100 per cent cotton, it is also available on silk dupion or taffeta to order. The fabric is available in six colourways, blue, pink, sage, lilac, coffee and black. Two colourways are available in Jacquard weave, and complementary check fabrics complete the range, creating a total look. Prices start from £27. Wallpaper and fine English bone china collections are also available.

Contact Details

Brian Lawrence
Tel: 01732 741308
Fax: 01732 450122
Website: www.brianlawrence.net

Distribution Showroom
Garin 1820
Chelsea Harbour Design Centre
London
SW10 0XE
Tel: 020 7351 6496

With over 25 years' experience in the interiors industry, Brian Lawrence has a reputation as an interior designer in tune with his clients' aspirations and being mindful of the environment in which his designs have to work. Projects undertaken range from modern, through traditional, to period-specific.

Brian Lawrence

From top: Crewel Golden Herb; Crewel Love in the Mist; Crewel Tree Peoney

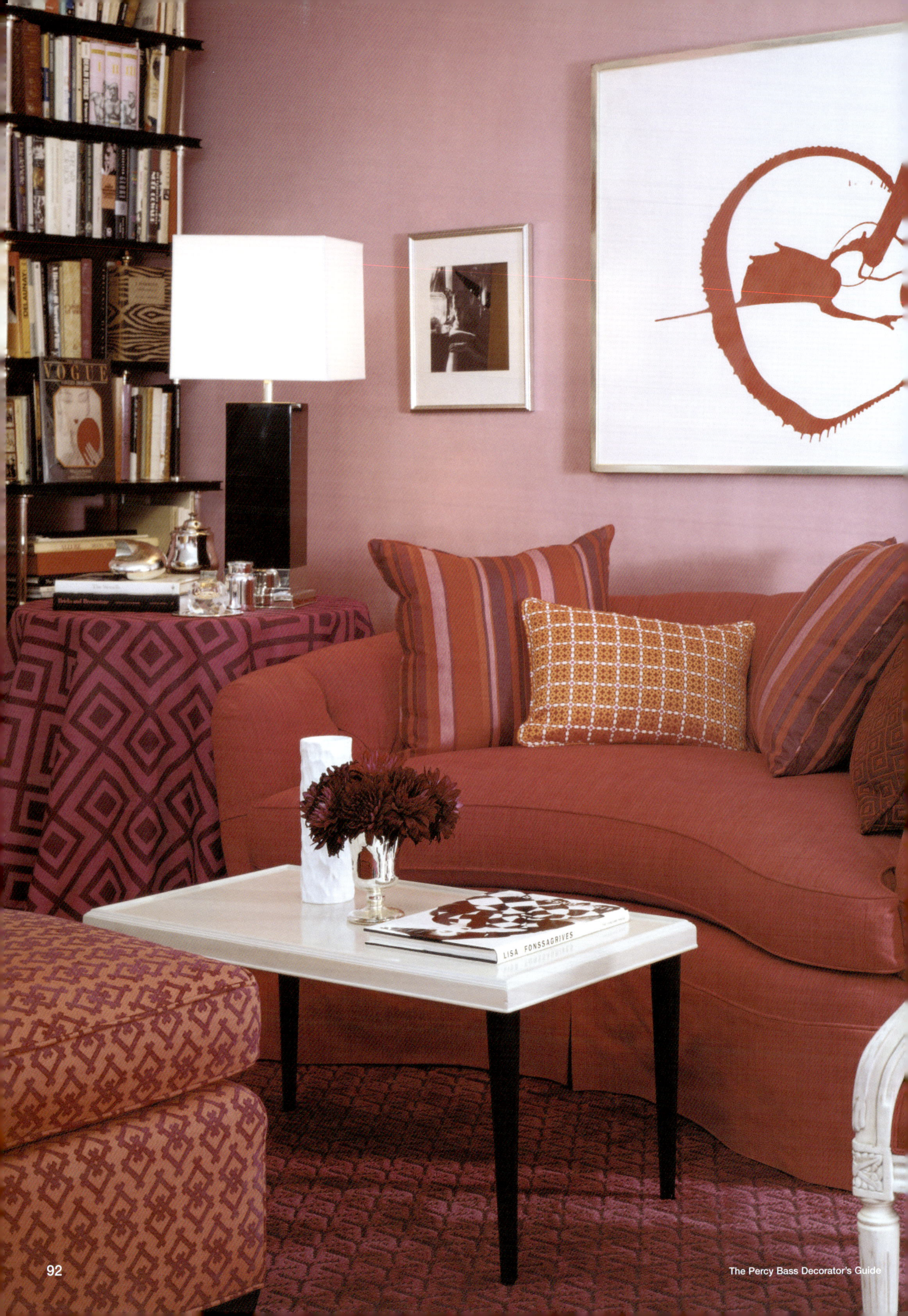
VOGUE
LISA FONSSAGRIVES

Lee Jofa

This company offers a truly transatlantic perspective on interior textiles, being formed by the merger of firms from the UK and USA.

A leading source of fine fabrics for almost two centuries, Lee Jofa is the result of a merger in 1965 of two great textiles companies: Arthur Lee Textiles, founded in England in 1888, and Johnson and Faulkner (later shortened to JOFA), established in New York in 1823.

With one of the largest and most beautiful collection of hand-blocked prints in the world, Lee Jofa continues to master the delicate harmony between past and future, tradition and innovation.

Groundworks is the contemporary brand of Lee Jofa representing the best of modern weaves, textures and prints such as the exclusive 'David Hicks by Ashley Hicks' collection, drawn from the famous David Hicks design archive.

Contact Details

Lee Jofa
Chelsea Harbour Design Centre
North Dome G18/19
London SW10 0XE
Tel: 020 7351 7760
Fax: 020 7351 7752

Head Office:
6 Stinsford Road
Poole
Dorset BH17 0SW
Tel: 01202 266800
Fax: 01202 266801
Email: sales@gpjbaker.com
Website: www.leejofa.com

One of the leading purveyors of elegant and refined furnishing fabrics on the market, and steeped in French textile history, this company has outlets in more than 40 countries worldwide.

Lelievre

In 1914 Henry Lelievre founded a small wholesale enterprise specialising in furnishing fabrics. In the 1940s and 1950s, Lelievre was renowned for the quality and texture of its fine velvets, but when demand for these was in decline by the 1970s, the company embarked upon an ambitious programme of diversification and investment. In 1972, the founder's grandson, Patrick Lelievre took over as president of the company (which he still is today) turning it into a true editor and creator of furnishing fabrics.

In 1973 the company purchased the historical mill of Quenin in Lyon, which specialised in silk furnishing fabrics (soierie Lyonnaise). Today Quenin is the principal weaving factory for Lelievre's own collections. The purchase of Tassinari & Chatel followed in 1997.

Contact Details

Lelievre (UK) Ltd
108-110 Chelsea Harbour Design Centre
London
SW10 OXE
Tel: 020 7352 4798
Fax: 020 7352 9569
Email: enquiries@lelievre.tm.fr
Website: www.lelievre.tm.fr

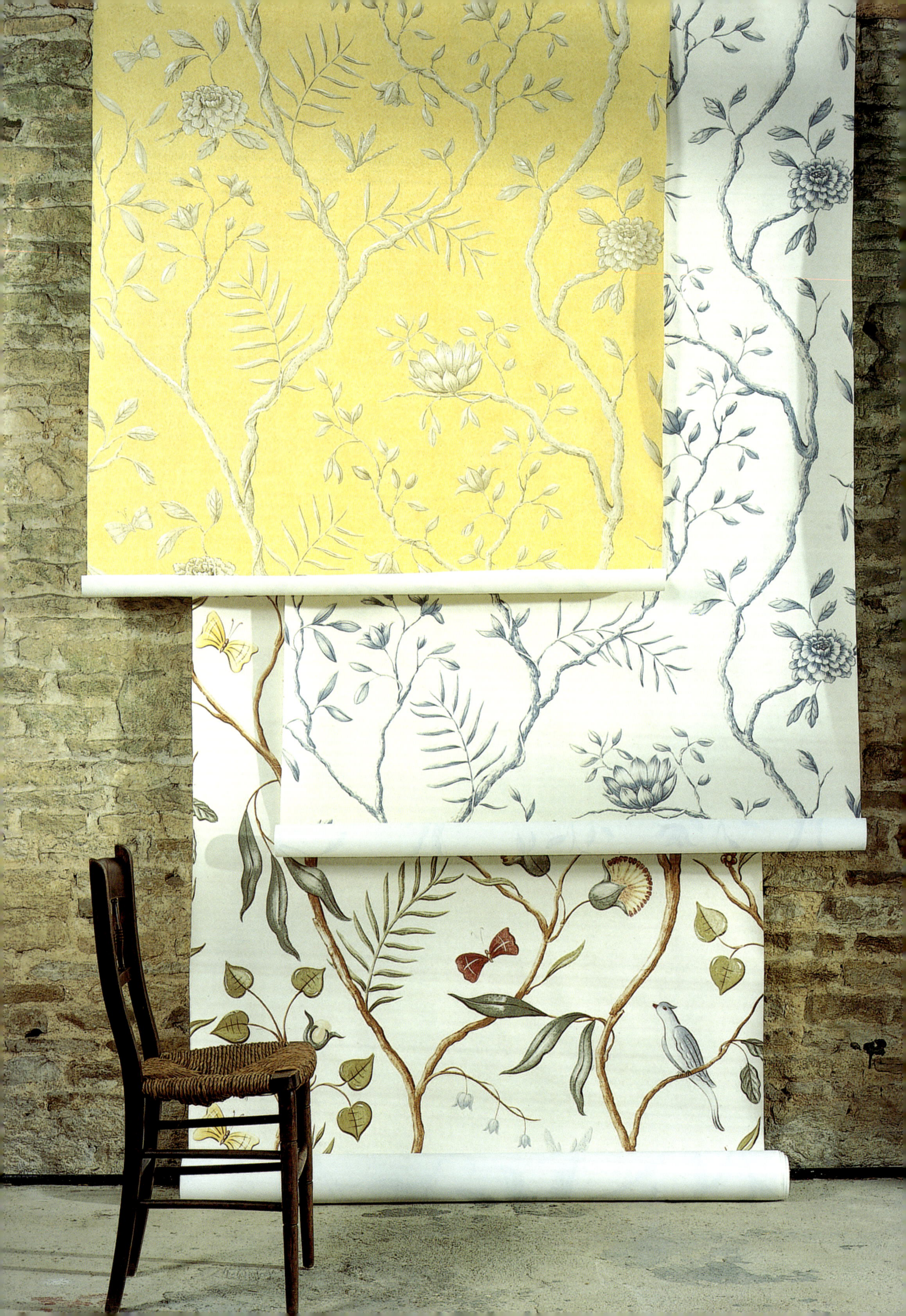

Lewis & Wood

A specialist in the production of fabrics and wallpapers, often incorporating print and dyeing finishes developed with its suppliers, Lewis & Wood can create beautiful fabrics and wall coverings to suit all tastes.

Lewis & Wood was started in 1994 by Stephen Lewis and the well known interior designer, Joanna Wood. The ethos of this company is that, as an independent textile and wallpaper maker, it has to make unique products that competitors don't have, and to that end it has developed a brand new concept in wall covering. Working with the decorative painter, Adam Calkin, Lewis & Wood has developed an extra-wide paper (132cm) that creates a stunning, large-format wall covering that looks terrific in both large and small spaces. These wall coverings have spectacular impact and give an expensive-looking, hand-painted effect. Calkin's designs are also printed on cotton and a jute/linen fabric, giving even more scope for using these wonderful, unique designs.

Opposite: Jasper Peony & Adam's Eden; Clockwise, from top left: Ivory Adam's Eden; Adam's Eden Fabric; Rose Jasper Peony

The Percy Bass Decorator's Guide

The company is well known for the sporting theme series of fabrics and wallpapers with wonderful, authentic images of horses, field sports and golfing. Character wallpapers were added to this series, featuring old visiting cards, calligraphy, botanical and maritime subjects. All the source material is carefully chosen, often using original engravings by well known artists of the period, such as Alken, Curtis and Samuel Gilpin. This provenance greatly adds to the interest and authenticity of the designs.

Lewis & Wood's collection includes toile de Jouy designs on both fabric and wallpaper, printed matelesse fabrics, and printed 100 per cent linen where special techniques gives fabrics, such as oxus, zarafshan and bruno, a vintage look and handle, while retaining the richness and depth of colour.

Contact Details

Lewis & Wood
5 The Green
Uley
Gloucestershire
GL11 5SN
Tel: 01453 860080
Fax: 01453 860054
Email: lewisandwood@lineone.net
Website: www.lewisandwood.co.uk

Showroom:
Borderline
Chelsea Harbour Design Centre
Lots Road
London
SW10 0XE
Tel: 020 7823 3567
Fax: 020 7351 7644

Clockwise from left: Hunting; Venetian Damask Linen & Wallpaper Chenille Sofa; Trade Cards; Opposite: Zarafshan armchair; French Linen Union roman blinds; Pimlico Stripe, Nantes, Oxus, Chinese Toile & Picardy cushions

The Percy Bass Decorator's Guide

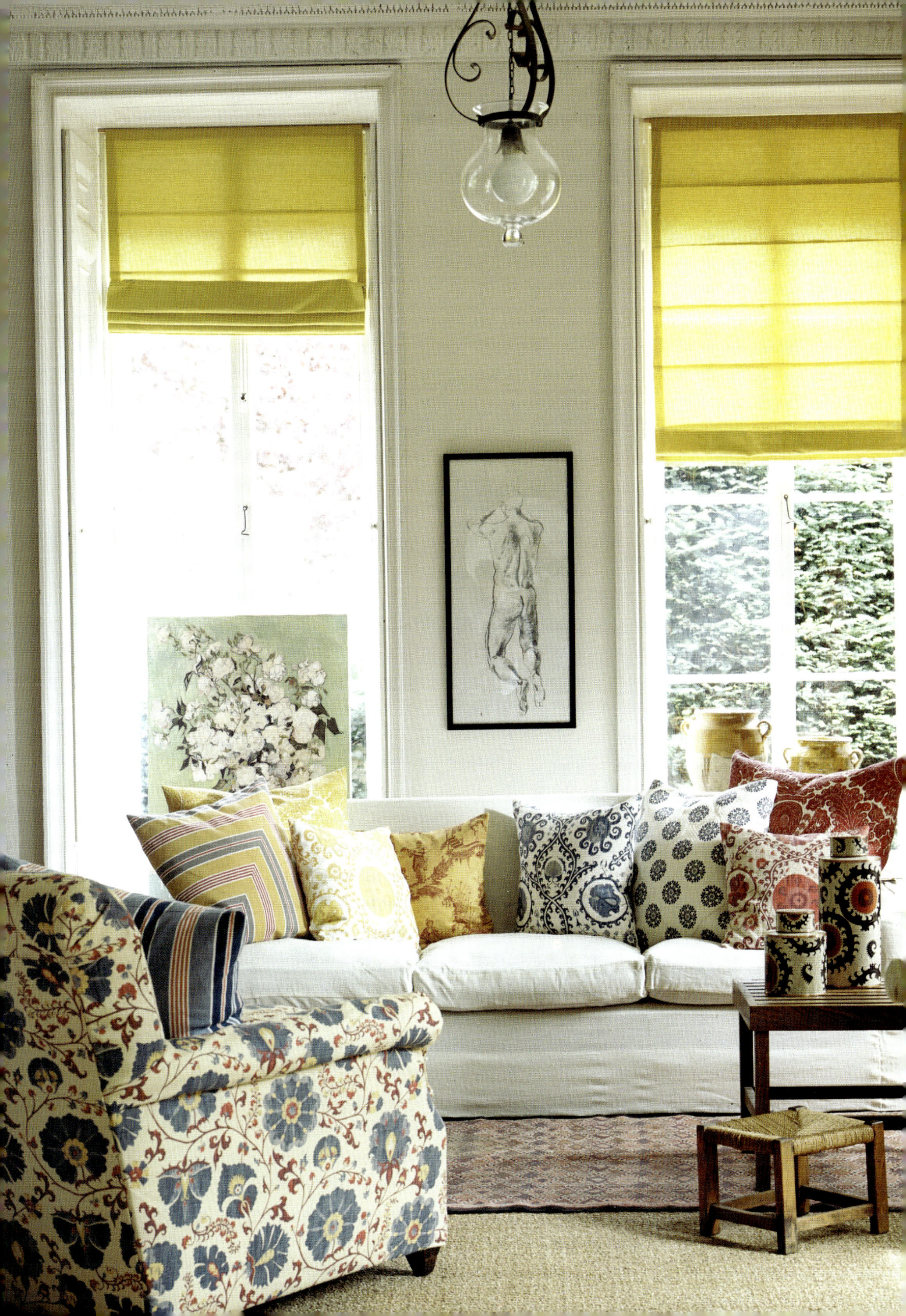

The Percy Bass Decorator's Guide

Linwood is a family-run business, with three generations of experience in the trade. Distributing abroad as well as in the UK, it has managed to maintain a personal touch even while operating on a worldwide basis.

Linwood designs and supplies exclusive weaves and prints for the furnishing and upholstery market, both here and abroad. Inspiration is drawn from a wide archive of documents and antique weaves as well as strong in-house design creativity.

Linwood markets thousands of fabrics as diverse as print, velvet, chenille, boucle, silk and dobby weave. The collection is truly diverse, spanning classic and contemporary styles with both plain and pattern designs. Particular attention is paid to the performance of the company's products with much of the range achieving contract specification for durability and flammability.

In addition, Linwood offers some of the finest leather hides available including heavy aniline, nu-buck and even American buffalo. These leathers may be specified onto an exclusive range of accessories including cubes, footstools and beanbags.

The company works closely with a small number of specialist weavers, printers and tanneries to create this exclusive collection. Linwood is supplied through an extensive network of carefully chosen distributors, interior designers and independent retailers. Such clients are served nationally by a dedicated team of Linwood sales executives.

Contact Details

The Linwood Fabric Company Ltd
15 Headlands Business Park
Salisbury Road
Ringwood
Hampshire
BH24 3PB
Tel: 01425 461176
Fax: 01425 461196
Email: sales@linwoodfabric.com
Website: www.linwoodfabric.com

Linwood

Opposite: Loxley; Above, from left: Skye; Somerley

Above: Malabar Paintworks. Malabar has brought together paint and fabrics in its paintcharts to provide ideas and inspiration for complete room schemes. The range is divided into five colour groups, with 21 colours per group to make choosing your paint and fabric an easy task; Top right: 'Dress' your walls with the China Grass Wallpaper range, shown here with chairs in Hana 01 from the Kuta Collection. These textural wallcoverings are made from sisal, paper, bullrush and rattan, and are ideal for drawing attention to one wall in a scheme; Bottom right: Faux suede stripe sofa, Niran 02, walls, Malabar Paintworks – thistle 63 and curtain, Mali 02 print from the Tasanee Collection

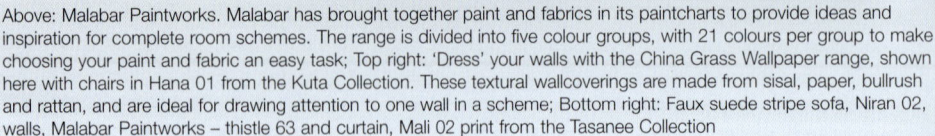

The Malabar Cotton Company

This company is well known for its handloom cottons, silks, delicate embroideries, sheers, checks and stripes suitable for all interior applications. Founded in 1985 in London, Malabar celebrates the abilities of hand weavers across India.

The first collection by Malabar, Bamboo, a ribbed plain cotton, remains one of its most popular ranges, and to meet the demands of today's clients, there are also ranges meeting high contract specifications.

To complement the extensive fabric ranges, Malabar recently launched a coordinating paint range, Malabar Paintworks, a collection of natural textured wall coverings, named China Grass, and a collection of striped cotton called Rugs and Runners. This was also the year that saw the launch of 12 new fabric collections, including crushed velvets, brushed plains, large-scale silk and linen damask, plain silks, textured naturals, linen prints and embroideries on cotton, and silk inspired by nature. The current Malabar range comprises nearly 50 collections with retail prices ranging from £5.50 to £105 per metre.

Malabar Paintworks

Malabar Paintworks features 105 classic and contemporary paint colours, taking inspiration from the stunning fabric collections. Each paint colour is paired with a complementary fabric, making it easy to create inspiring room schemes.

All colours are available in matt paint (2.5l £24.99) and multi-surface satin paint (750ml £14.95). In addition to supplying stockists across the UK, Malabar is distributed throughout the world in 40 countries, and since 2002 has shown in 14 showrooms across the USA.

Contact Details

The Malabar Cotton Company
31–33 The South Bank Business Centre
Ponton Road
London
SW8 5BL
Tel: 020 7501 4200
Fax: 020 7501 4210
Email: info@malabar.co.uk
Website: www.malabar.co.uk

Marvic is well known for its luxury weaves, rich silks, archive prints, stripes, toiles de Jouy, soft, silky chenilles, velvets and moirés.

Marvic Textiles has a well-established reputation for quality upholstery weaves of great style and distinction. Enduring classic fabrics such as Pine Tree, Clover, Renishaw and Tulipan feature widely in both town and country homes as well as in many contract situations. Indeed, two Prime Ministers have been photographed sitting on Pine Tree/Clover!

The toiles de Jouy range currently offers 25 beautiful designs. They include typical pastoral and neo-classical images, but also included are architectural, Chinese-style and illustrative designs. Furthermore, six of the most popular designs are available as wallpapers in colours to coordinate with the fabrics.

The nine silk collections offer a wide range of beautiful silk qualities, including classic Italian damasks, taffeta stripes, checks and plains, intricate floral embroideries, and contemporary floral, damask and semi-plain designs in lightweight silk qualities.

The Marvic range is marketed exclusively to interior designers and design professionals and the company has many years' experience of working with specifiers and supplying the luxury hotel market. Marvic Textiles offers a highly personalised service to customers, with great care and attention to detail. Most orders are immediately available from Marvic's London warehouse and it offers an efficient, rapid delivery service worldwide. The fabric and wallpaper ranges are available through interior designers, specialist shops and department stores.

Contact Details

Marvic Textiles
G26 Chelsea Harbour Design Centre
London
SW10 0XE
Tel: 020 7352 3119
Fax: 020 7352 3135
Email: sales@marvictextiles.co.uk
Website: www.marvictextiles.co.uk

Marvic Textiles

This long-established family-owned business offers a wide and versatile range of classic fabrics with a contemporary twist. Quality, elegance and glamour are the hallmarks of this company's style.

From left: Pemberley Fabrics and Wallpapers; Imperiale Collection; Metro Two and Fantasia; Terpsichore; Toiles Anciennes

Curtain, Bead-Chocolate DPF251, in bowl, Bead-Ochre DPF253 and Ochre DPF282, interlocking, on table, Coral-Sand DPF260
Inset: Back cushion, Coral-Ochre DPF262, Drift-Sand DPF271;
Opposite: Top cushion, Drift-Chocolate DPF275, bottom cushion, Bead-Chocolate DPF25
Inset, from top: Curtain, Coral-Pearl Blue DPF261, fabric in basket, Twist-Pearl Blue DPF291; curtain, Drift-Chocolate DPF275, chair, Drift-Sand DPF271, front cushion, Bead-Chocolate DPF251, stool, Bead-Sand DPF250; curtain, Drift-Ebony DPF276, cushion, Coral-Ebony DPF264

Natasha Marshall

An innovative approach to pattern will enhance any interior. Natasha Marshall's elegant and simple geometric design work has gained the recognition of leading architects, interior designers and retailers worldwide.

Natasha Marshall's designs have evolved from photographs of city architecture, abstract shapes that play on the use of colour, texture and space. The strong signature fabric and wallcovering ranges are all distributed worldwide by Today Interiors Ltd. Colours range from deep walnuts, rich coppers and charcoals through to soft, fresh mint, light ochres, crystal blues and sands.

Extensive stocks are held in the UK for immediate dispatch, and the company is proud to be respected for its high standard of quality and customer service.

Prices range from £30 to £55.

Contact Details

Natasha Marshall
Distributed by Today Interiors Ltd
Hollis Road
Grantham
Lincolnshire
NG31 7QH
Tel: 01476 574401
Fax: 01476 590208
Websites: www.today-interiors.com
www.natashamarshall.com

From top: Bottna fabric by Anna Danielson; Lumimarja fabric by Erja Hirvi; Afrikan Kuningatar fabric by Oiva Toikka

Marimekko

Putting Finnish frocks on the map in the 1960s with a collection made famous by Jacqueline Kennedy, this innovative company has become an institution and a Scandinavian design classic.

Marimekko was founded in 1951 in Helsinki, Finland by Armi and Viljo Ratia. They recruited the most innovative and daring textile designers of the time to create an identity that clearly reflected the spirit of modern Finnish design. Vuokko Nurmesniemi, Maija Isola and Annika Rimala are just a few of the Marimekko talents that have made design history.

The radical designs soon made Marimekko an outfit for leaders in the pop and art world. In 1960, the first Marimekko retailer in the USA ordered some dresses for his small shop in Cape Cod. Jacqueline Kennedy saw them and bought the entire collection. 1960 was the year John F Kennedy was elected president and the new first lady presented herself to the press in her modern, uncomplicated Finnish frocks. This was the beginning of the first Marimekko craze, with exposure in all the leading fashion magazines.

Modern classics

The founders of Marimekko had a vision of 'total design' and joyful, uncomplicated living. Today this still means bold and colourful textiles, casual clothes in simple cuts and distinctive patterns that are instantly recognisable as Marimekko. New fabrics are added each season in cotton drill, batiste and linen and can be used for curtains, blinds and special upholstery.

Marimekko has become a Finnish institution and a Scandinavian design classic. New talents are now joining, such as Anna Danielsson and Erja Hirvi. The opening of a Marimekko shop in the UK confirms the spirit and soul of this unique lifestyle brand.

Contact Details

Marimekko
Shop
16/17 St Christopher's Place
London
W1U 1NZ
Tel: 020 7486 6454
Fax: 020 7486 6456

Marimekko
Agent & Wholesale
UK and Republic of Ireland
Skandium Ltd
Tel: 020 7486 2309
Fax: 020 7486 6456
Email: maria@marimekko.co.uk
Website: www.marimekko.co.uk

Contact Details

Christopher Moore Studio
(by appointment only)
48 Cromwell Avenue
Hammersmith
London W6 9LA
Tel: 020 8741 3699
Email: info@thetoileman.com
Website: www.thetoileman.com

A leading specialist in authentic reproductions of eighteenth- and early nineteenth-century fabrics, most notably toiles de Jouy, Indiennes and indigo prints, Christopher Moore also offers a comprehensive make-up and decoration service and specialises in handmade quilts, dressing antique French beds, curtains, cushions and lampshades.

Matching choice

The company currently has the largest choice of toiles de Jouy on the market, with over 50 designs, all with matching papers. New designs in all the collections are continually being added.

Retail prices for fabrics range from £35 to £65 (plus VAT) per metre. Retail prices for papers from £55 (plus VAT) per 10 metre roll.

Christopher Moore

Also known as The Toile Man, this specialist in eighteenth- and early nineteenth-century fabrics has an unparalleled choice of toiles de Jouy with matching wallpapers.

Mulberry Home was launched in 1991 in response to demand from customers who not only wanted to buy bags and accessories but also wanted to enjoy the complete Mulberry approach.

The Mulberry Home range, which aims to combine the best of English heritage with a blend of warm opulence and cool contemporary style, has developed into a much sought-after lifestyle brand, encompassing fabrics, soft furnishings, wallpaper, glass, china and furniture.

Contact Details

Mulberry Home
Chelsea Harbour Design Centre
North Dome G18/19
London SW10 0XE
Tel: 020 7351 7760
Fax: 020 7351 7752

Head Office:
6 Stinsford Road
Poole
Dorset BH17 0SW
Tel: 01202 266800
Fax: 01202 266801
Email: sales@mulberryhome.com
Website: www.mulberry.com

From fashion to furnishing, Mulberry has taken its unique style into the home with this range of interior products.

Mulberry Home

Left: Gheisha
Below: Donovan's Chinese Lady

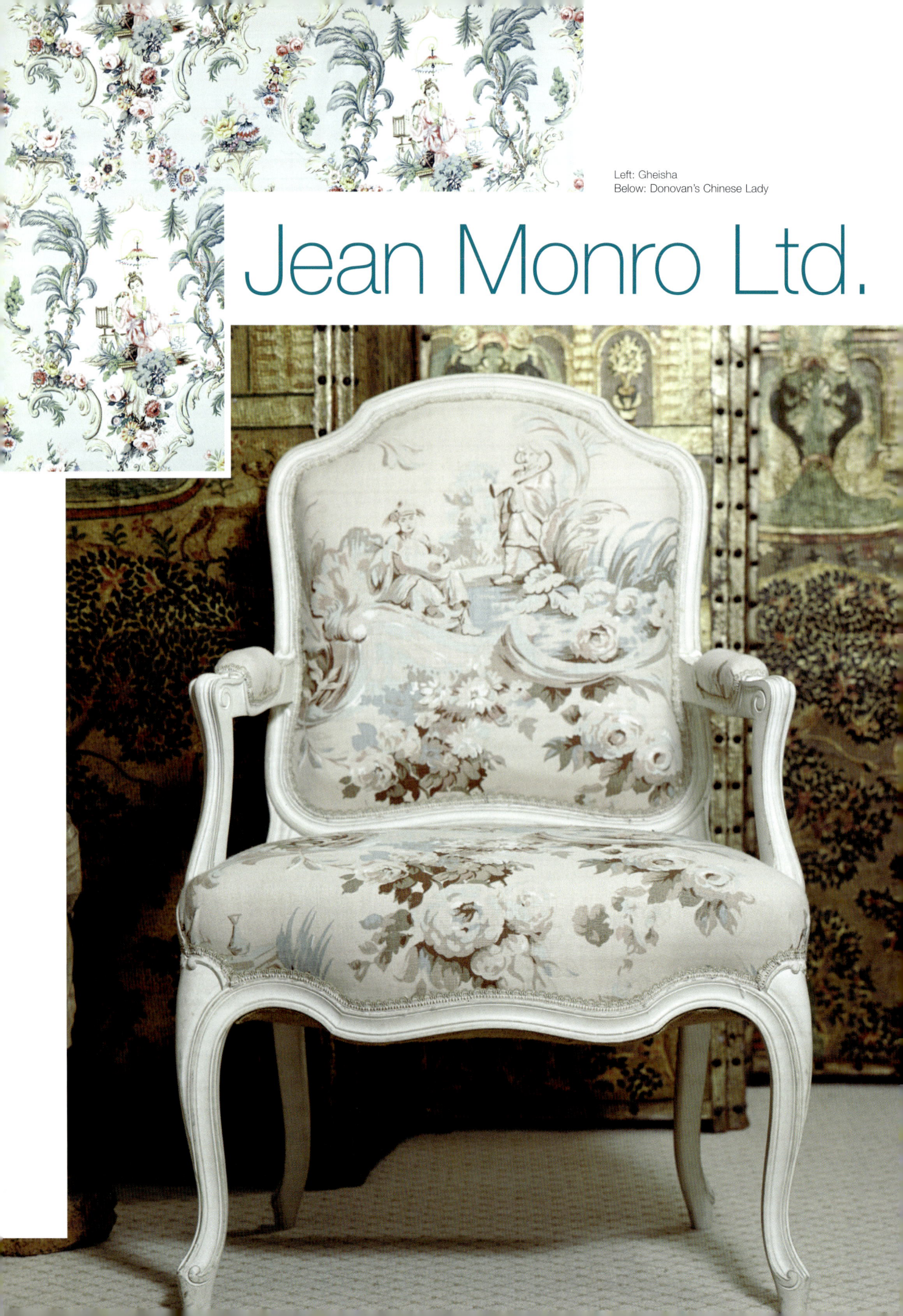

Jean Monro Ltd.

This company is justly renowned for English traditional printed chintzes and linens, produced from archive material printed in England on the finest cloths, nowadays not necessarily chintz. There are no compromises in production: if 24 screens are needed for the best result, 24 screens will be made.

In 1981 Jean Monro, daughter of the famous London decorator of the 1920s Mrs Geraldine Monro, decided to reproduce and market the favourite designs her mother had used over the years, some of which were already produced exclusively for the decorating company. Thus Jean Monro Design came into being.

Turnell & Gigon purchased the company in 1998 and the 'Design' was dropped from the name to avoid confusion with the decorating company.

Hand-block printing
Jean Monro is one of the very few companies still editing hand-block designs. This process requires an apprenticeship of seven years, often involves hundreds of different blocks and naturally takes a long time to produce. However, it creates a look that cannot be satisfactorily copied by any other printing method.

The Hazelton House collection contains probably the finest hand-blocks still in production and, when added to the existing Jean Monro blocks, this means that Jean Monro holds probably the largest range of hand-blocked fabrics in Europe.

Below (left to right): Lemoine; Polyanthus

Recent collections include:
- Beauchamp – a floral design of English cottage garden flowers printed on a soft linen union.
- Jean – named after the founder of the company and redrawn from a woodblock of 1855.
- Laetitia – a fine 100 per cent silk taffeta.
- Hollyhock hand-block – a large-scale bouquet of hollyhocks hand-blocked on heavy 100 per cent linen.

Contact Details

Jean Monro Ltd.
T&G Group of Companies
Chelsea Harbour Design Centre
Lots Road
London
SW10 0XE
Tel: 020 8971 1712
Fax: 020 8971 1716
Email: sales@jeanmonro.com
Website: www.jeanmonro.com

Kiev, a contemporary re-interpretation of a bobbled tieback originally made for the Russian imperial court

Henry Newbery & Co Ltd

Over 200 years of continuous trading, an astonishingly rich archive and the wholehearted embrace of contemporary design assure Henry Newbery a unique place in the world of interior decoration.

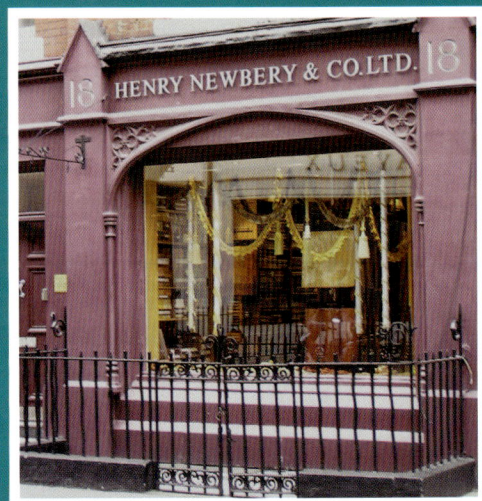

Left: Chic contemporary trimmings in bronze from the Jazz Age Collection;
Below: Fenice, sleek double tasselled tiebacks from the Venezia Collection, in Sovereign and Platinum colourways

embrace the use of unusual weaving techniques and radical textural combinations. Glass, metal, wood and crystal are also employed. In-house facilities for the creation of bespoke trimmings have been expanded and the company has also acquired the exclusive UK and Irish distribution rights for Johannes Wellmann furnishing fabrics.

Recent commercial contracts include a number of fashionable boutique hotels and high-profile opera, ballet and film productions. Henry Newbery has established itself as a truly iconic brand, forward-looking, yet drawing inspiration from its own unique heritage. It is an invaluable resource to interior designers and soft furnishers.

Contact Details

Henry Newbery & Co Ltd
18 Newman Street
London
W1T 1AB

Trade contact details
Pauline Ellis
Clem Malone
Tel: 020 7636 5970
Fax: 020 7436 6406
Email: sales@henrynewbery.com
Website: www.henrynewbery.com

In 1782 John Newbery, an itinerant weaver from Berkshire, moved to London, where he began weaving and selling furnishing trimmings at 54 Upper Marylebone Street. The business prospered and moved to larger premises in Percy Street, an area teeming with soft furnishers and furniture makers. Here the family lived and worked for more than 100 years. Skilled workers created elaborate fringes, braids, cords and tassels for use in grand public buildings, stately homes and the theatre.

The company traded throughout World War II under Allen Newbery, until 1944, when the factory was bombed. Sadly, the old looms, stock and archives were destroyed. Undaunted, Allen revived the business as a furnishing trimmings wholesaler when peace was restored. Carol, his eldest daughter, began work in 1953, and successfully developed the designer, contract and export markets.

In 1986 the company moved to its present location at 18 Newman Street, close to its West End roots. The showroom, office, stock and samples are all accommodated in this building. In July 1955 Henry Newbery was honoured with a Royal Appointment to HM Queen Elizabeth II, which was renewed in 2000.

Clem Malone became Sales Director in 2000 and now oversees the running of the business. New design directions

The Percy Bass Decorator's Guide

Northcroft Fabrics specialises in fine fabrics, designed for domestic and contract use and for both upholstery and soft furnishings. Offering a large and exclusive selection of classic velvets, damasks and silks, the company launches new collections each year.

Northcroft Fabrics

From rich, striped velvets and elegant, floral damasks to intricate Chinoiserie-styled silks, Northcroft epitomises the best in textile quality. Small but expert in its field, Northcroft provides a personal and knowledgeable service for its customers as well as a cutting service.

The velvets in the collection are perfect for curtains and upholstery. There is a choice of plain (Rochelle), semi-plain (Cadiz) and embossed velvets (Dampierre), available in cotton, linen, mohair, silk or mixed piles. For those requiring contrasting and complementary fabrics, there are a number of choices, including Dampierre and Seville or Sans Gene which are all antique linen velvets in similar colour options.

The Northcroft Fabrics range of damasks has a classical, timeless appeal. Typically inspired by traditional Italian, French or English designs from the sixteenth and seventeenth centuries, they feature patterns on a grand scale in rich fabrics, which are well-suited to curtains, upholstery and soft furnishings such as Acanthus and Medici.

Northcroft Fabrics has an extensive range of silks with both contemporary design and classical appeal, such as Horsham, a modern botanical Jacquard and Nanking, a traditional Chinoiserie design. Spitalfields, the floral English silk, has the extra dimension of being reversible. These silks are suited to curtains and soft furnishings.

Northcroft Fabrics supplies retailers, interior designers and specifiers on a trade-only basis in the UK. Trade prices range from £24 to £190 per metre.

Left: Medici in terracotta gold, pure silk; Above: Limoges and Loire in brick red, cotton/modacrylic damask; Below: Dampierre and Seville in beige, linen velvet

Contact Details

Northcroft Fabrics
Highfields
Grubwood Lane
Cookham Dean
Berkshire SL6 9UD
Tel: 01628 488700
Fax: 01628 484949
Email: sales@northcroftfabrics.co.uk
Website: www.northcroftfabrics.co.uk

Above: Bellissimo CS 100 per cent trevira cs (8 colours available) ca.180cm wide; Inset, from top: Malibu, 60 per cent viscose, 40 per cent cotton (4 colours available) ca. 145cm wide; Alameda, 35 per cent cotton, 35 per cent polyester, 30 per cent viscose (9 colours available) ca. 140cm wide; Contura, 70 per cent silk, 30 per cent polyester (8 colours available) ca. 330cm wide; Andorra, 50 per cent polyester, 30 per cent acetate and 20 per cent silk (7 colours available) ca. 135cm wide; Gira & Girlanda, 60 per cent viscose, 40 per cent acrylic (8 colours available in each) ca. 140cm wide

nya nordiska

From bold decorative patterns to subtle neutrals in upholstery, sheer, soft furnishing and curtain-weight fabrics, this company have remained at the forefront of innovative interior textile design. Producing a diverse and eclectic mix of contemporary and classic fabrics, often incorporating unconventional materials, keeps the collections fresh, alive and exciting.

nya nordiska, which literally translates as 'new nordic' is famous for innovation and avant-garde design. Since the company was founded over 40 years ago by Heinz Röntgen in Düsseldorf, Germany, it has received numerous design awards which are a testament to the company's reputation for excellence in product design and of delivering superior quality. The company, based in Dannenberg, Germany, has worldwide distribution with dedicated showrooms in London, Paris, Tokyo and Como, Italy.

Originally inspired by Swedish design during the 1960's, this German company has over 600 fabrics in its contemporary collection. Bold decorative patterns and subtle neutrals in a variety of natural fibres and up-to-the-minute synthetics are available in a vast palette of colours and textures. These even include classic upholstery and curtain-weight velvets produced in fashionable vibrant colours as well as natural shades and sharp monochrome black and white patterns.

Sheers feature considerably in the nya nordiska collection, several of them available in widths up to 330cm, which can be railroaded to create a seamless run of fabric. An eclectic mix of materials including a silk and bamboo viscose blend, metallics, wools, crisp cottons and quality linens, some of them embroidered, create a stunning, luxurious and desirable environment. Pretty Swarovski crystal motifs glisten on a smooth double-weave sheer fabric, complimented by a popular range of pleated and scrunched sheers.

nya nordiska launch a new collection in the Spring and Autumn of every year to ensure that they remain at the forefront of innovative interior textile design.

Contact Details

nya nordiska textiles ltd.
2/26 Chelsea Harbour Design Centre
London
SW10 0XE
Tel: 020 7351 2783
Fax: 020 7352 5305
Email: britain@nya.com
Website: www.nya.com

The Percy Bass Decorator's Guide

The Percy Bass Decorator's Guide

Opposite: The Mimi collection of coordinating weaves
Above, from left: The Casselmae, Melbourne and Rosina collections

Nouveau Fabrics

High-quality classic prints, beautiful colours and attention to detail have given this family business a worldwide reputation for producing elegant fabrics, trimmings and wallpapers.

Contact Details

Nouveau Fabrics Ltd
Queens Road
Doncaster
South Yorkshire
DN1 2NH
Tel: 01302 329601
Fax: 01302 341489
Email: sales@nouveaufabrics.co.uk
Website: www.nouveaufabrics.co.uk

Nouveau Fabrics is a small family business based in Yorkshire that has consistently created fine furnishing fabrics since 1972. Products are designed and coloured in the company's studio by Katherine Beaumont and Nigel Thompson. Known for classic prints and beautiful colour ranges, the company has recently diversified into more contemporary products with the same attention to detail that has become its hallmark. Fabric collections are often complemented with ranges of specially designed trimmings to add a personal finishing touch.

Nouveau has distributors worldwide and supplies most good retailers and interior designers. Its average retail fabric price ranges between £22 and £38 per metre.

The Percy Bass Decorator's Guide

Nursery Window

Printed in England, these quality fabrics are original and versatile, and are not limited to the nursery. Themes range from oriental to New World and are popular on both sides of the Atlantic.

Located in Walton Street for the last 20 years, Nursery Window is a brilliant find for those looking for exclusive and imaginative fabrics. Although it is primarily known for children's fabrics, its range is by no means limited to the nursery.

The latest fabric from Nursery Window, Imperial Garden is a prime example of the originality and versatility of the range. This oriental theme can be used anywhere in the house, as part of a formal dining room or a luxurious bedroom design.

In an era of mass production and outsourcing to far and wide places, Nursery Window goes against the grain by insisting that all fabrics are printed in England. One feel of the fabric is enough to tell that only the best quality will suffice. As a result, excellent fabric is produced, not only for curtains and accessories but also fabric that can be used to upholster sofas and other items of furniture.

Another Nursery Window print, New World, is extremely popular with customers both in the UK and the USA. This fabric portrays a voyage of discovery and although an imaginative and intricate design, the fabric lends itself to many room settings and is both relaxing and pleasing to the eye.

Contact Details

Nursery Window
83 Walton Street
London
SW3 2HP
Tel: 020 7581 3358
Fax: 020 7823 8839
Email: info@nurserywindow.co.uk
Website: www.nurserywindow.co.uk

Left: Tristan & Dorabella fabric;
Opposite, from top:
Tours Rosebriar Wilton runner;
Duoline fabric; Tapis rug

The Percy Bass Decorator's Guide

The philosophy of Roger Oates has always been to create floor coverings that his customers can relate to – simple yet comfortable with an undeniably modern twist – and it is a principle that has paid off. The designs are now favourites with internationally famous interior designers and regarded as the contemporary way to complement hard flooring. The company is expanding this theme with a collection of furnishing fabrics that have been created for the individual who refuses to compromise on pure quality and sophisticated simplicity, and who appreciates function and practicality.

Rugs and runners
Stair runners, in both wool flatweave or cut and pile Wiltons, are a refreshing alternative to natural floor coverings, and far more chic and dramatic than ordinary stair carpet. The narrow widths can be invisibly joined to create area rugs and wall-to-wall fitted carpets. Bold, sensitively coloured stripes add drama, whilst narrow stripes add a textural quality to both rugs and runners, giving a timeless appeal whilst creating a lasting impression. Prices for flatweaves start at £75 per linear metre, Wiltons from £80 per linear metre.

Contemporary rugs are individually made in luxurious mouflon cloth. The Tapis, a woven, heavily felted, brushed wool, is available in a choice of natural, rich and bright colours, joined and edged with a blanket stitch detail to create a variety of modular designs. Prices for runners start at £385, rugs from £360.

Relaxed modernity
The fabric collections have a fresh, contemporary look that instantly says style and modernity but at the same time is relaxed and easy to live with. Trademark stripes – from simple, crisp, smooth lines through sophisticated, soft tonal bands to large-scale textured bars of voluptuous colour – give them an individual look, in hand-woven cottons or the latest high-tech fibres. The fabric ranges truly extend the Roger Oates style within any interior. Prices for fabrics start at £20 per metre.

For those in search of pure quality and sophisticated simplicity with a modern twist, these stunning floor coverings and fabrics are in demand with leading interior designers worldwide.

Roger Oates

Contact Details

Roger Oates
1 Munro Terrace
Riley Street
London SW10 0DL
Tel: 0845 612 0072

The Long Barn
Eastnor
Ledbury
Herefordshire
HR8 1EL
Tel: 0845 612 0153
Email: sales@rogeroates.com
Website: www.rogeroates.com

Today, Les Olivades carries on the tradition of fabric printing begun in Provence three-and-a-half centuries ago. The company offers its customers:

- A range of printed and woven fabrics for house decoration, sold by the yard, or made into products such as curtains, blinds, net curtains, sofas, throws, bedspreads and cushion covers
- Bed linen, including sheets, duvet covers and pillowcases
- Tableware products such as tablecloths, napkins, placemats and coated fabrics
- Accessories matching the fabric collection, including dishes, lamps, sofas, chairs and small pieces of furniture

Les Olivades

This French company offers its clients a wide range of printed and woven fabrics, drawing on techniques of fabric printing that go all the way back to the sixteenth century.

Top: Rectangular tablecloth Ansouis; Above, (from left): Armchair La Begude, sofa throw Rega and l'Oustau, cushion cover l'Oustau; Square tablecloth Fruchie; Left: Square tablecloth Aubenas

Contact Details

Les Olivades
Registered office
Chemin des Indienneurs
13103 St Etienne du Gres, France
Tel: +33 4 90 49 19 19
Fax: +33 4 90 49 19 20
Email: comexport@les-olivades.com
Website: www.les-olivades.com

Agent (UK)
Frits Kortenbout
20 Goodliffe Gardens
Tilehurst, Berks
RG31 6KZ

Store (UK)
Percy Bass Ltd
184 Walton St
London
SW3 2JL

The Percy Bass Decorator's Guide

Fabrics Silk Empire collection
from left: 180435H – 33
Permisson; 80072H – 219
Cinnamon; 80091H – 06 Gold

Duralee Fabrics is based in Bayshore, New York. Having celebrated its 50th anniversary in 2002, Duralee is now the fastest-growing decorative fabrics company in the USA. Its success is based on:

- Innovation. Many of the woven designs are designed by and produced exclusively for Duralee. The majority of the print collections are exclusive.
- Variety of products. There is a range to suit every taste and style, from the finest sheer to the heaviest contract upholstery, and everything in between.
- Continual development. Duralee is currently launching an average of 70 new collections every year.
- Longevity and service. The ranges are supported by considerable depth of stock, and each collection has several years' continuity.

Orchard Fabrics Ltd is proud to be the exclusive distributor in the UK for Duralee Fabrics.

Contact Details

Orchard Fabrics Ltd
Unit 2 Avondale Industrial Estate
Avondale Road
Edgeley
Stockport
Cheshire
SK3 0UD
Tel: 0161 477 4225
Fax: 0161 429 0993
Email: orchardfabrics@btconnect.com

Orchard Fabrics

Innovation, variety, development and service are integral to the success of this fabrics company.

The Percy Bass Decorator's Guide

A selection of Emma P's latest range including Isla Check, Clementine and Provence Stripe

Emma P Fabrics

Emma Purcell trained in Paris for three years and her inspiration has been predominantly taken from nineteenth-century French designs. The range incorporates a varied use of yarns, instantly recognisable to the touch. Colour has also played a vital part in the design process where Emma has used stunning combinations that will both enhance and complement any interior.

The weaving process starts by importing the natural fibres which originate from cotton plantations in India, and silk worm farms in China. Once they arrive at the mill, the yarns are quality checked and then washed and dyed. Once this has been completed the yarns are ready to be used and woven into the fabrics that you see today.

The latest range incorporates linen, cotton and silk which are produced in England on Jacquard looms. There are a total of four designs in ten different colourways. Aside from the standard range which incorporates over 40 different fabrics, Emma P Ltd also undertakes special commissions whereby the colours can be changed and woven in any colour combination for a minimum order of 10 metres.

An independently owned fabric company, Emma P specialises in bespoke woven fabrics suitable for curtains and upholstery. The company was founded by Emma Purcell who has produced a range of fabrics that will sit comfortably in either a contemporary or traditional interior.

Contact Details

Emma P Fabrics
134 Lots Road
London
SW10 0RJ
Tel: 020 7349 7044
Fax: 020 7351 5044
Website: www.emmap.co.uk

Connecticut Blue

Luxury White Collection

Lexington Glace

The Percy Bass Decorator's Guide

Opposite and below: A selection of carpets from Schumacher, exclusive to Tim Page Carpets

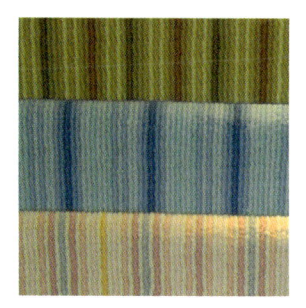

Tim Page Carpets

From concept to final fitting, Tim Page Carpets takes care of everything. With an exclusive range and even custom-made designs, the perfect carpet is provided to suit every customer's requirement.

With over 20 years of experience in the carpet industry, Tim Page guides customers through the whole process of choosing a new carpet. For most people this is one of the most important decisions they will take, as carpet covers large areas and is very long lasting.

With a vast range of stock carpets, some from exclusive agencies, customers will find a carpet to suit all rooms and styles. Tim Page Carpets can offer carpets for both modern and traditional interiors, from pale neutrals to the deepest hues, velvet piles to textured surfaces, wool carpets to coirs and sisals, plains to motifs and checks.

However, if wall-to-wall carpet is not right, rugs can add a further dimension to any interior or add warmth to wooden floors. Tim Page Carpets can make a wide selection of custom-made rugs bordered in a choice of jute, linen or leather bindings in a wonderful array of colours. Runners on staircases look particularly striking and these come in a wide selection of designs and widths.

Expert help
Once customers have selected a carpet they can leave the rest to Tim Page Carpets. If required, the company can organise measuring and then its expert fitters will install the carpet, leaving clients confident from start to finish.

If customers cannot find the perfect design, Tim Page Carpets will create one. Taking inspiration from a painting or perhaps a detail from a curtain fabric, the company can design a carpet – almost anything is possible.

For the future Tim Page Carpets will continue to look for new and innovative qualities and designs to add to its collection.

Contact Details

Tim Page Carpets
T & G Group of Companies
Chelsea Harbour Design Centre
Lots Road
London
SW10 0XE
Tel: 020 8971 1714
Fax: 020 7349 8835
Email: tim@timpagecarpets.co.uk
Website: www.timpagecarpets.co.uk

The Percy Bass Decorator's Guide

Parkertex

Parkertex, with a newly expanded range of collections for classic and contemporary interiors, offers fabrics across a wide range of textures and scales.

Contact Details

Parkertex
Chelsea Harbour Design Centre
North Dome G18/19
London SW10 0XE
Tel: 020 7351 7760
Fax: 020 7351 7752

Head Office:
6 Stinsford Road
Poole
Dorset BH17 0SW
Tel: 01202 266700
Fax: 01202 266701
Email: sales@gpjbaker.com
Website: www.gpjbaker.com

The name Parkertex is derived from Parker Knoll Textiles. Parker Knoll, a company historically famous for its fireside chairs and recliners, was also the holding company for a number of other enterprises including G P & J Baker.

The Parkertex range has been added to significantly with the recent launches of several new and exciting collections. It now offers a huge variety of eclectic and versatile fabrics with a fantastic range of texture and scale.

Easy to work with and competitively priced, Parkertex fabrics sit beautifully in any interior environment, classic or contemporary, and are also perfect for contractual use.

The Percy Bass Decorator's Guide

A useful source for exclusive fabrics, William Potts Limited also stocks the finest reproduction furniture. The comprehensive fabric collection includes traditional prints, linens, silks, chenilles, piques, naturals, stripes, checks, upholstery weights, as well as some doublewidths and washable ranges. All collections are available from stock and are for trade only. Contemporary lines including acetates have been particularly well received.

Reproduction furniture

The furniture shown is by Moissonnier whose collection is recognised as being unique. These exceptional products are new creations inspired by the eighteenth century, in vibrant colours and finishes all made by hand in France.

The company also acts as agent for Massant, a fantastic Belgian company specialising in reproducing eighteenth-century furniture and decorative items. Art Deco and other twentieth-century styles are now available.

Contact Details

William Potts Ltd
Unit 47
Smithbrook Kilns
Cranleigh
Surrey GU6 8JJ
Tel: 01483 274 778
Fax: 01483 276 766
Email: williampotts@supanet.com

Above, from left: Pink dot chenille, ref. Rivoli col 5,145cm width, viscose/cotton; Monkey fabric, ref. Palm Springs – Curry, 140cm width, 34cm repeat, 100 per cent cotton; 2 striped silk, ref. Bangalore col 4, 140cm width, 100 per cent silk

William Potts Limited

From traditional prints, linens and silks to contemporary acetates, a fine array of fabrics is complemented by handmade reproduction furniture. This ranges from eighteenth-century to Art Deco and other twentieth-century styles.

Pink commode, ref. 573 Louis XV Commode by Moissonnier, 85cm height x 130cm width x 63cm depth, Laquée Rosé

Green commode, ref. 573 Louis XV Commode by Moissonnier, 85cm height x 130cm width x 63cm depth, Laquée

Pongees Silks

This silk specialist has been established for over 70 years and has achieved an excellent reputation as one of the UK's foremost suppliers of high-quality silk fabrics to trade-only customers. Based in Hoxton, London, this company is at the cutting edge of both contemporary and classic design.

Pongees excels in offering a complete service to the interiors trade. With an in-house stock collection of over 170 silk fabrics, it offers one of the most comprehensive range of furnishing qualities in the UK. The range includes the most delicate of chiffons, georgettes, iridescent and metallic organzas, through to satins, taffetas, shantung and textured weaves, to trend-inspired, in-house designer Jacquards and British wovens.

The collection is constantly growing, reflecting the ever-changing tastes, colours and influences in the interior design industry. With no minimum order, Pongees Silks prides itself on being the discerning designer's first-choice silk fabric house. The extensive range on offer is available in a collection of catalogues and books and is supported by an experienced sales team as well as agents and distributors worldwide.

Pongees is able to commission individual designers, exclusive embroidery and beading designs with a minimum run of just 20m. Custom dying and weaving starts at a minimum of 100 metres. Special finishes such as flame proofing can also be undertaken. Through years of experience and a long list of manufacturers and contacts around the world, designers have found Pongees invaluable when sourcing new colours and qualities of silk fabrics.

Top left and right: Hoxton collection;
Above: Odello collection

Contact Details

Pongees Ltd
28–30 Hoxton Square
London
N1 6NN
Tel: 020 7739 9130
Fax: 020 7739 9132
Email: info@pongees.co.uk
Website: www.pongees.co.uk

The Percy Bass Decorator's Guide

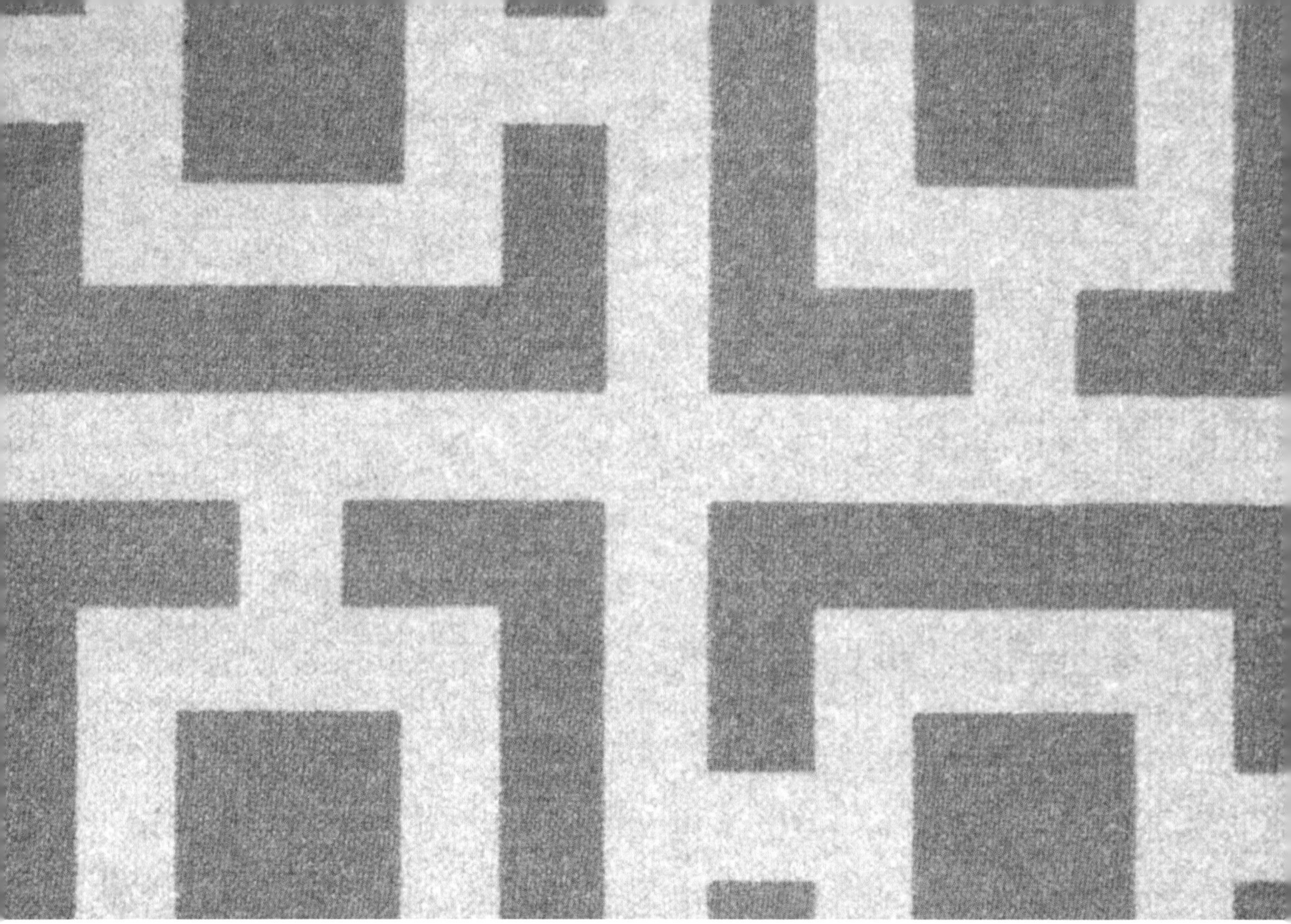

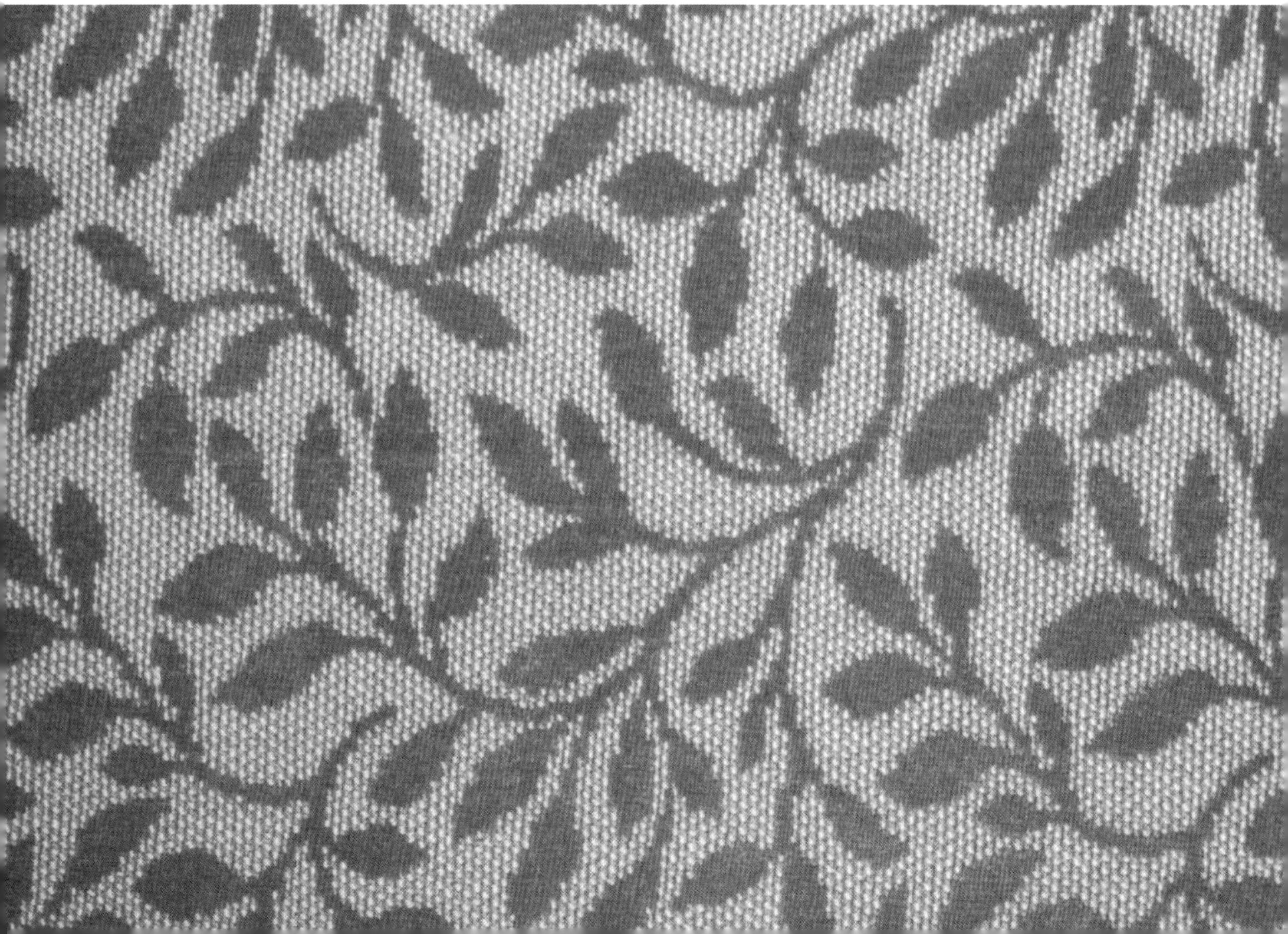

PWC International Ltd

This family-run business specialises in producing the finest bespoke woven carpets for the interior design trade. Providing custom-designed carpets, the perfect carpet can be created in every style and colour as well as a range of textures.

PWC International Ltd specialises in producing the finest quality traditionally woven bespoke carpets for the interior design trade. With an enormous archive of designs, the ability to dye yarns to any colour and a wide range of yarns and textures, the design possibilities are endless. CAD prints and hand trials (strike offs) of selected designs can be produced for client approval prior to weaving the designs in either broadloom (over 100m²) or narrow width and on Wilton or Axminster looms.

PWC can also make the designs as hand-tufted rugs or in some cases convert them into carpet tiles for contract locations. PWC offers a full planning, estimation and installation service and has many years of experience in installations ranging from domestic to large contract projects. PWC also exports to many locations worldwide.

Contact Details

PWC International Ltd
Studio 3
Fairbank Studios
Lots Road
Chelsea
London
SW10 0RY
Tel: 020 7349 7440
Mobile: 07770 755807
Email: enquiries@pwcinternational.co.uk

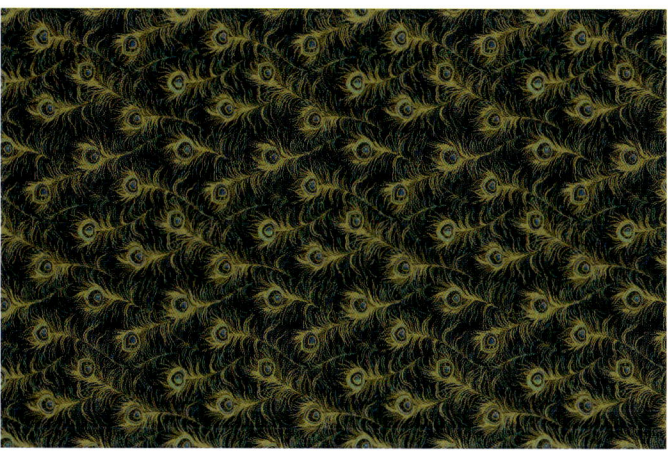

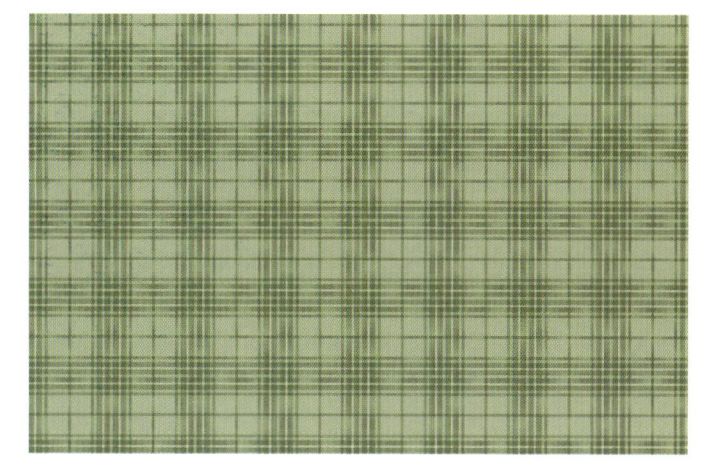

From left: Reymondon Osier, single tieback 111020-001 only available in Ecru; Reymondon Osier Carnival 111021 available in 15 colours; Reymondon Medicis 112345, available in 15 colours

Reymondon Trimmings

With an exclusive range and an enormous archive from which clients can choose designs and colours, this company has a steadfast reputation for high-quality trimmings.

Contact Details

Reymondon Trimmings
Frits Kortenbout
20 Goodliffe Gardens
Tilehurst
Berkshire
RG31 6FZ
Tel: 0118 941 1593
Fax: 0118 941 8205
Mobile: 07802 224 667
Email: frits.kortenbout@virgin.net

Established as Reymondon Trimmings early in the twentieth century, the company changed its name to Lyon Manufacture Passementerie in June 2004, and retains its reputation, built up over many years since its inception, for producing quality trimmings at reasonable prices.

Within its vast collection it has a variety of bullion fringes, tassel fringes, braids, key tassels, fan edge fringes and, of course, ropes of various diameters.

The mill has a vast archive from which designs can be chosen and also produces lines in bespoke colours and designs.

Colours are based on design colours selected from companies such as Pierre Frey, Nobilis, De Lorca, Belvilacqua and Lelievre.

Style E35

This company's high-quality Portuguese tapestry rugs are made from pure New Zealand wool. The small selection is constantly being updated, and rugs can be designed for interior decorators or clients with a specific room in mind.

Deborah Rolt Rugs

Style C10

Style E32

Deborah Rolt's rugs made exclusively for her by a family-run firm in Portugal, whose expertise has been handed down through the generations. All rugs are hand-stitched using pure New Zealand wool. They are extremely thick and have proven over the years to be exceptionally hard wearing.

Only a small selection of designs are shown in the brochure and website. Deborah is constantly updating the designs so that they are in line with modern styles and colour trends.

Made to match
Rugs can be designed for a particular scheme – colours, patterns and sizes changed to meet specific designs – and Deborah works closely with interior decorators or directly with clients so that each rug is custom made for the room. Prices range from £225 (including VAT) for a 2ft x 3ft rug to £5955 (including VAT) for a 10ft x 14ft rug. Designs can be made up in any size or colour.

Contact Details

Deborah Rolt Rugs
66 Howards Lane
Putney
London
SW15 6QD
Tel: 020 8780 5288
Email: anne@deborahroltrugs.co.uk
Website: www.deborahroltrugs.co.uk

Sandberg textiles depict 12 Swedish lighthouses together with their coordinates, so any sailors who have the urge can use them for navigation

Sandberg

This Swedish company is introducing a new pattern to its collection, the hand-printed 'Vinga – Svenska Fyrar', based on the Vinga lighthouse. Other textile designs in the range are inspired by nature.

Sandberg, founded in 1976, designs and manufactures wallpaper and fabrics. The company exports to some 40 countries. Since 1996 Sandberg has been supplying interior designers and decorators in the UK and Eire on a daily basis, direct from Sweden.

Scandinavian motifs

Along the very long coasts of Sweden, in the east, south and west, there are many beautiful old lighthouses, which today are a priceless part of Swedish cultural heritage. The Vinga lighthouse, which has long been the guiding beacon for ships journeying to Göteborg, has lent its name to the new hand-printed textile. Sweden's national poet, Evert Taube, whose father was the lighthouse master at Vinga, grew up on the island where the lighthouse stands. His songs are incomparable expressions of a sailor's longing for the sea, but also of his longing to return back home, his desire to see the flashing lighthouse just outside his own harbour.

Sandberg textiles depict 12 Swedish lighthouses together with their coordinates, so any sailors who have the urge can use them for navigation. The edge is decorated by signal flags conveying the message that this is the Sandberg handprint 2005. Previous textiles in this series of exclusive hand-printed textiles are Althea, designed by Hanna Wendelbo-Hansson, with hollyhock motifs, and two textiles inspired by the Finnish artists the von Wright brothers: Swedish Birds (Georg), designed by Daniel Langelid; and Scandinavian Fish (Wilhelm), designed by Pia Artling.

Contact Details

Sandberg Tyg & Tapet AB
Box 69
523 22 Ulricehamn
Sweden
Tel: +46 321 531660
Fax: +46 321 531661
Email: sales@sandbergtapeter.se
Website: www.sandbergtapeter.com

The Percy Bass Decorator's Guide

The Silk Gallery

A company born out of necessity, The Silk Gallery has been able to supply a young generation with imaginatively designed fabrics and continually evolving styles.

When interior designer Kathryn Horbye found it difficult to find exactly the fabrics she and her clients wanted, she started her own design company. The silks then available were damasks drawn from historical documents and, although elegant, they were too unimaginative for her younger clientele who wanted to define their own generation with a more glamorous and fun interpretation of design. She opened the Silk Gallery in 1993 in what was then the fledgling Chelsea Harbour Design Centre.

From the outset, Kathryn decided that all her fabrics would be made in the UK to keep the traditional weaving industry alive. Her first collection of hand-printed designs and woven taffetas were drawn from architectural prints in 100 per cent silk. She later discovered that double weaves (pocketed cloths), where polyester threads are interspersed between silk yarn ensures durability without destroying the look and texture of pure silk. This process diminishes the risk of fading.

Subsequent collections focused on Kathryn's sharp eye for evolving trends interpreted in a subtle, pared down, classical style, which looks elegantly sophisticated but at the same time up-to-the-minute. These sumptuous fabrics sit equally well with antiques or contemporary furniture.

Adding trimmings to the range has proved popular, as they coordinate with the collections. These can be stock items or bespoke. A minimum order of 8 metres applies for custom-coloured fabrics and trimmings.

Kathryn's latest collection includes Othello, a strong, large-scale, art deco-influenced silk with geometric coordinates, the diaper pattern of Casio and the multi-coloured, striped Ariel. Venice is a textured, large-scale damask, with the raised silk threads shimmering on a cotton base.

The colour combinations are exquisite: celadon/cream, chocolate/sage/red and taupe/blue on an ivory ground with a hint of mulberry. They offer ultimate inspiration for those wishing to give their home a makeover.

Top, from top left: Venice gold/beige with Napoleon twist fringe; Silk Damask Andromeda & Comet Stripe, Constellation pony tail tie back; Antique Green; Above: English Rose Campari

Contact Details

The Silk Gallery
25 Chelsea Harbour Design Centre
London
SW10 0XE
Tel: 020 7351 1790
Fax: 020 7376 4693
Email: silkgallery@dial.pipex.com

Maltster Eau de Nil on a Nene Sofa
Inset, from top: Shiraz Ember, Cellini Firebird, Temperance Brick

138

The Percy Bass Decorator's Guide

The classic style of the Ian Sanderson collections was created in 1964 by Ian Sanderson, who had a vast knowledge of textiles and weaving techniques. The company is now run by his son, Julian and his wife Helen is the designer and stylist. The quality of this showroom's output is superb as well as being competitively priced.

Plain weave ranges like Crosby, Panne and Jasper are in a colour palette to suit all tastes and they fit in well with the classically inspired and evolving feature fabrics. Damask, florals, stripes and checks blend rather than coordinate to produce a total look.

The company was the first to take traditional French mattress ticking covers into the interior design world, initially producing it in five colourways. These are used for sofas, cushions and linings, and over the years the design and colour range has progressed in line with fashion.

Current collections include a classical linen print, in beautifully blended colours such as thyme, teal and persimmon, which forms part of the range called Ad-Infinitum, so called because fabrics in different colours and textures can be added to it. In the New Hampshire weaves range there is an innovative woven patchwork which cleverly combines a check and trailing vine co-ordinate designs.

One of Ian Sanderson's current features is a range of leather trimmings. These consist of plaited or shaped tiebacks, laced braid and leather piping cord for sofas or cushions. It comes by the metre with invisible joins, and is a bright idea for a make-over to sharpen up an existing room.

Right: Caverson Leather Trimmings
Below: Panne Grape on a Hollesley Sofa

Contact Details

Ian Sanderson (Textiles) ltd
P.O. Box 148
Newbury
Berkshire RG20 9DW
Tel: 0870 458 1579
Fax: 0870 458 1589
Email: sales@iansanderson.co.uk
Website: www.iansanderson.co.uk

Ian Sanderson

A family business now in its second generation, Ian Sanderson offers an exclusive range of beautifully designed fabrics at competitive prices.

The Percy Bass Decorator's Guide

Allegra double tasselled tieback on a formal curtain;
Opposite: Allegra tassel and a selection of custom trimmings

All of Smith & Brighty's passementerie is made in a factory in Portugal in the traditional way, some on original hand looms. Marion Smith and Jane Brighty, who run their showrooms in Washington and London respectively, started the business in 1985. They took over an established company that had been supplying the Portuguese market since 1930.

Both Marion and Jane were impressed by the exceptional quality of this intricate decorative art produced by a workforce who between them had decades of experience. They initially brought the products to London where they were sought after by discerning interior decorators looking for something different and exquisite. Smith & Brighty trimmings were used for the refurbishment of Windsor Castle after the disastrous fire, as they were able to reproduce damaged items precisely in design and materials.

Although trimmings can be custom-made in exact shades to match any colour scheme, Smith & Brighty also holds a large selection of stock items that can be delivered quickly. Pattern books are also available with coordinating collections including one that matches the fabrics from the Gainsborough Silk Weaving Company.

Smith&Brighty

With over 20 years' experience in the decorative art of passementerie, tassels, fringes, braids, ropes and tiebacks, this company provides trimmings custom-made to match any fabric in any colour. Items can be pulled directly from a vast collection held in stock.

Contact Details

Smith & Brighty
Jane Brighty
Office 1
Ground Floor
Fairbank Studios
75–81 Burnaby Street
London
SW10 0NS
Tel: 020 7351 1221
Fax: 020 7351 6622
Email: smithbrightytrim@btconnect.com
Website: www.smithandbrighty.com

The Percy Bass Decorator's Guide

142

Opposite: GSD has built up a reputation for its strong colour palette, attention to weave detail and texture
Right, from top: A selection of fabrics from the new contemporary collection; Close-up detailing of the weave construction

George Spencer Designs

George Spencer Designs was established in the 1940s. Initially trading as a company of interior designers, the company expanded into designing and manufacturing its own collections of fabrics, trimmings and wallpapers.

George Spencer Designs' fabrics include cotton checks, stries and documented linen prints as well as a contemporary collection of zesty wools, muted cashmeres, earthy mohair velvets, striking stripes and sophisticated silks. These innovative fabrics incorporate the very latest in technology and design.

The range of textures and colours make them suitable for both traditional and contemporary use. For example, the checks are in subtle colour combinations. Used traditionally, they are perfect for lining four-poster beds or the backs of chairs. For contemporary use, they are ideal for cushions, roman blinds, walling or covering sofas. The mohair velvets would look equally stylish on a classical sofa finished with a coordinating George Spencer Designs bullion fringe, or on an angular contemporary sofa on tapered feet. The difference is in the colour choice, the palette ranging from classic neutrals to strong, clear colours, such as quince and tango. All the fabrics are available immediately from stock.

George Spencer Designs also operates as an interior design company offering a comprehensive service.

Trimmings
George Spencer Designs offers a comprehensive collection of trimmings, all

Left: Mimi fringe, available from stock and woven using wool, chenille and mercerised cotton; Opposite: GSD wallpapers are all hand blocked, made to order and can be custom-coloured

available from stock. The collection is constantly expanding and to date consists of five collections, four of which are manufactured in mercerised cotton, which gives a luxurious soft sheen to the finished designs. The Trimmings Collection III is manufactured in 100 per cent wool, making it perfect for tapestries, linens and more matt finished fabrics.

Designs include ropes, fan edges, picot braids, walling braids, chequer board braids, block fringes in various lengths with or without fan top header details, tassel fringes, scalloped fringes, onion fringes, banner weight bullion fringes, roll top bullion fringes, pom pom fringes, tassel tiebacks, rosettes, key tassels and button tufts.

The colour palette has been painstakingly blended and mingled so that it complements a huge variety of fabrics. In some cases as many as 28 colours have been combined to create one colourway. Across the range of trimmings manufactured in mercerised cotton there are a total of 40 colourways available.

Collection III, the wool collection, is available in seven colours, including evergreen, sour green, claret, pomegranate, amber, sky and cream. The designs range from braids and decorative fringes to bullions in either 5in or 8in depth. Tiebacks and accessories complete the collection.

In addition to the stock collections, a bespoke service is available. This service is incredibly popular and allows clients to select their own designs and have them colour-matched exactly to their chosen fabrics. The designs vary from a simple, custom-made picot braid woven in the client's individual colours to elaborate fringes and tassels incorporating hangers and scroll gimp detailing originating from eighteenth-century designs. The bespoke service by George Spencer Designs is efficient and professional with competitive lead times.

George Spencer Designs is proud of the fact that all its trimmings are manufactured in the UK.

Wallpapers
George Spencer Designs produces a beautiful collection of hand-blocked wallpapers. The wallpaper collection evokes the spirit of early, intricate craftsmanship with its range of designs. The collection features designs in the style of early European papers; each produced using techniques and materials which date back to the seventeenth century.

Reminiscent of the work of the Arts and Crafts movement, wallpaper designs feature organic, botanical forms in pastel and muted shades.

George Spencer Designs has also revived the art of producing historically accurate flocked wallpaper by using a wool flock rather than the manmade fibres currently utilised throughout the industry.

As part of the process, carved blocks are used to print the design one colour at a time. With the use of different shades and colours, a floral design may be printed using 16 or more separate blocks. The colours are all made from natural pigments.

All designs can be custom-coloured to clients' individual requirements.

Contact Details

George Spencer Designs
33 Elystan Street
London SW3 3NT
Tel: 020 7584 3003
Fax: 020 7584 3002
Email: sales@georgespencer.com
Website: www.georgespencer.com

Founded because of a shared passion for the English Renaissance, Stuart Interiors, and its textiles division, Stuart Renaissance, offer restorations and re-creations of interiors from a range of historical periods.

Stuart Interiors

Stuart Interiors was founded 29 years ago, when a group of furniture makers and designers, all with an interest in the period from 1500-1730 broadly known as the English Renaissance, joined forces. Today, the aim of Stuart Interiors (named after the era in British history), is to offer a complete period interior design and manufacture service, restoring or re-creating interiors dating from the medieval to the late eighteenth centuries, to include architectural joinery, furniture, lighting, antiques and, importantly, textiles, working both at home and abroad.

Stuart Renaissance Textiles
Based in the heart of the Somerset countryside, Stuart Renaissance designs and weaves faithful copies of early English and European fabrics ranging from the Byzantine period to the nineteenth century. Many of the designs have not been woven for hundreds of years and were rediscovered with the help of the museums of Europe. As a result of this research the company offers an exciting range of fabrics known as the 'Renaissance Collection'. These include worsted and pure silk damasks, brocatelle, lampas

Contact Details

Stuart Renaissance Ltd
T/A Stuart Interiors
Barrington Court
Barrington
Ilminster
Somerset
TA19 0NQ UK
Tel: 01460 240349
Email: design@stuartinteriors.com
Website: www.stuartinteriors.com

and double cloths in wool, silk, cotton and linen. Where practical, the weaves are constructed as they would originally have been.

Stuart Renaissance Textiles also produces original designs in the traditional style of the period and is pleased to offer this service to anyone wishing to create their own ambience.

The Argyll Lodgings, Stirling, Scotland
In 1995, consultants from Stuart Interiors were appointed by Historic Scotland to work alongside Historic Scotland's own experts on the refurbishment of the principal rooms at the Duke of Argyll's Lodgings.

Meetings with Historic Scotland at Stirling, together with lengthy discussion and an in-depth study of the surviving inventories, resulted in the decision to furnish the house as it may have looked in 1680. Stuart Interiors prepared a portfolio for each area, detailing the specification for items to be replicated. All aspects of interior decoration were covered. Of particular interest are the textiles, which include wall hangings, bed and furniture upholstery.

Mentioned in the inventory as 'stamped stuff', it was evident that most of the furnishing textiles were of this original type of woollen cloth. A rare surviving example of its type may be found in Knole House, Kent. Stuart Interiors' consultants ascertained the nature, composition and method of manufacture of the material in order to replicate it, along with all the appropriate trimmings.

Following the successful completion of this project, Stuart Interiors has also provided consultants for a restoration currently underway of the Royal Apartments at Stirling Castle, once again to include textiles, lavish 'Cloth of Gold' and heavily embroidery-embellished silk damasks and velvets. Once the palace is completed, with its fine furniture and magnificent textiles it will be the only royal residence in Europe to appear as it may have looked when it was originally furnished, offering a glimpse of royal life 450 years ago.

Other historic textile commissions include Gainsborough Old Hall, Birmingham Town Hall, the Foreign Office, Warwick Castle, Leeds Castle, the Victoria & Albert Museum's British Galleries and the National Portrait Gallery.

As part of Stuart Interiors, Stuart Renaissance Textiles has as its showrooms the idyllic setting of Barrington Court, near Ilminster in Somerset, a large Elizabethan manor house with medieval origins, belonging to the National Trust. It is a showcase for Stuart Interiors, both as a standing example of interior restoration expertise and as a home for the enterprise.

Above: English needlework, typical of the early 1720s and representative of the dress and furnishing fashions of the day. Woven in cotton and worsted yarns;
Far left: Luccese silk from the fourteenth century (and woven again during the gothic revival). Adapted in the form of a double cloth, woven in wool and linen;
Left: The Duke of Argyll's Lodgings;
Below: Abbeville, circa 1650. Originally a double cloth in linen and cotton, shown here in wool and linen

Contact Details

Tassinari & Chatel
distributed by Lelievre (UK) Ltd
108–110 Chelsea Harbour Design Centre
London
SW10 OXE
Tel: 020 7352 4798
Fax: 020 7352 9569
Email: enquiries@lelievre.tm.fr
Website: www.lelievre.tm.fr

Tassinari & Chatel was founded in 1680 in Lyon and its emblem, the griffon, recalls the original millsite in Lyon, 'le quartier du Griffon'. The Pernon family's client list reads like a who's-who of European royalty, including Louis XIV, Catherine II of Russia, Queen Marie-Antoinette, Charles III and IV and Gustav III of Sweden.

The post-revolutionary period in eighteenth-century France was a time of artistic and technological innovation, with originality in the designs of Philippe de Lasalle and formidable technological advances by Joseph Marie Charles dit Jacquard, the engineer who designed the loom which still bears his name today and which completely transformed the methods of producing figured silks.

The nineteenth century saw the thorough refurbishment of France's palaces and, after visiting the celebrated factories in Lyons, Napoleon appointed Pernon as sole fabric supplier. The new 'Empire' style of fabric design found its way into Les Tuileries, Versailles, Fontainebleau, and subsequently into export markets.

In the twentieth century the skills and knowledge of Tassinari & Chatel have proved invaluable in the reproduction of original designs for Versailles, The Elysée Palace, Fontainebleau and The White House.

Today, this heritage of over 100,000 original archives is available for reproduction and a selection of the Patrimoine Collection, which is a compilation of around 700 designs from Louis XIII to the twentieth century, can be viewed at the Lelievre showrooms in Paris and London.

Tassinari & Chatel

Founded by the Pernon family, the firm of Tassinari & Chatel is the fruit of generations of textile excellence passed on in the spirit of dynastic tradition. It is renowned for its historical and classical elegance, including silk damasks, silk brocades, silk velvets and warp-printed silk taffetas.

Established in 1977, this family business specialises in the creation and design of custom-made trimmings such as curtain tiebacks, stair ropes, bullion fringes and decorated chandelier supports. All trimming designs are created to meet the shade requirements and individual design instructions of the customer. Based in the heart of Lancashire with its long tradition of spinning and weaving, the company has, over the years, grown both in stature and reputation to become one of the UK's leading manufacturers in this field.

With a typical lead time of only three weeks and small minimum order quantities, the option of having customised trimmings has rarely been so accessible.

Furnishing trimmings are created for traditional settings (as illustrated) whilst for more contemporary schemes, feather trimmings and tassel tiebacks with a combination of aluminium and leather are coloured to a client's specifications.

Dr Brian J. Taylor & Son

Expert in the creation of customised trimmings, this family business based in the heart of Lancashire has an impressive client base and a reputation to match.

Contact Details

Dr Brian J. Taylor & Son
Chadwick Street Mill
Blackburn
B132 4AA
Tel: 01254 691010
Fax: 01254 691022
Email: canyoudothis@tasselsandtrimmings.com
Website: www.tasselsandtrimmings.com

Above, from: Grand Rubens tieback, overall tassel length 30cm; Standard and specially made tieback finials

The Percy Bass Decorator's Guide

Above: Imperial Tassel Fringe; Below: Examples of custom trimmings created to match a client's own fabric, 'Lady Rose' by Bernard Thorp & Co.

The workforce is one of highly skilled and dedicated people trained to the company's own exacting standards. When needed the company also employs a wider skill base of wood turners and specialist yarn dyers, all of whom are based in England and meet its quality criteria.

Drawing on these vast talents Taylor's has successfully produced custom-made trimmings for foreign embassies, boutique hotels and bespoke upholsterers, in addition to innumerable private residences both in the UK and overseas.

Utilsing this custom trimming service is simplicity itself and there is no unrealistic minimum order quantity to curtail your ideas. In fact, a minimum order of just two items of tassel tiebacks or five metres of bullion fringe will suffice.

Once contacted, Taylor's can offer a comprehensive mail order colour-matching service. In this, after submitting fabric samples and colour swatches along with a list of trimming requirements, design outlines will be produced to meet explicit instructions. Drawing on its extensive range of dyed stock yarns, colour-matched wrappings of yarn together with examples of individually made trimmings will be speedily sent for client approval. Work will only commence when the client's complete satisfaction is achieved.

For the client's peace of mind and the company's enviable reputation, owner Chris Taylor will personally prepare all custom-made trimming proposals and oversee the creation of clients' exclusive trimmings prior to delivery by courier.

The Percy Bass Decorator's Guide

Titchfield

Mixing historical references with contemporary attitudes, Titchfield offers a complete design service, including upholstery in its own workshop as well as curtain making.

Catriona Swaffer started working as an interior decorator in the 1980s before working with Tissunique, commissioning fabric designs for the historic house market. With this experience she built up considerable knowledge of traditional design.

In the 1990s, she worked independently developing her own fabrics. Her first fabric, called Court Stripe, was an embroidered silk taffeta.

She specialises in embroidered fabrics based on silk, cotton and linen. Another embroidered design is Mimosa, an embroidered border on a linen cloth. Inspired by historical documents, the colourways and scale were Catriona's own idea.

The company also produces toiles de Jouey, including an exotic scene called Danse Egyptienne and another called Chatsworth. These are printed in France, in inky red, blue, green and purple. Coordinating with these are open linen checks, which were originally intended to cover furniture as case cloths in the eighteenth century. The Volunteer Chintz design, a military composition of mounted soldiers, tents, soldiers on parade and stagecoaches, has been widely used in houses with an Irish background.

Inspired when working as a guest designer in a silk mill in Bangalore, India, a tone-on-tone sunflower silk damask was created in ivory and stylish chocolate brown with a 1930s look.

Fascinated by children's samplers from the 1950s, Catriona's new collection, called Hoola Hoops, is made up of embroidered borders depicting enchanting scenes. The collection has matching plains, an open check and a print called Topsy Turvy. All are on natural linen. This charming and fun collection can be easily adapted for childrens' rooms as well as discerning adults.

In 2000, Catriona and her husband Keith took over the interior design shop Schemes in the Notting Hill area of London. As well as housing their own workshop, it is also the window for Catriona's fabric collections.

Contact Details

Titchfield
16 Needham Road
London
W11 2RP
Tel: 020 7727 3775
Fax: 020 7792 0294
Email: mail@schemesinteriordesign.co.uk

Opposite, from left: Yo-Yo, vertical border from the Hoola Hoops collection; Catch me, all-over design on natural linen;
Above: Topsy Turvy, patterned print from the Hoola Hoops collection
Below, from left: Dancing Boy, embroidered vertical border from the Hoola Hoops collection; Coordinating check from the Hoola Hoops collection

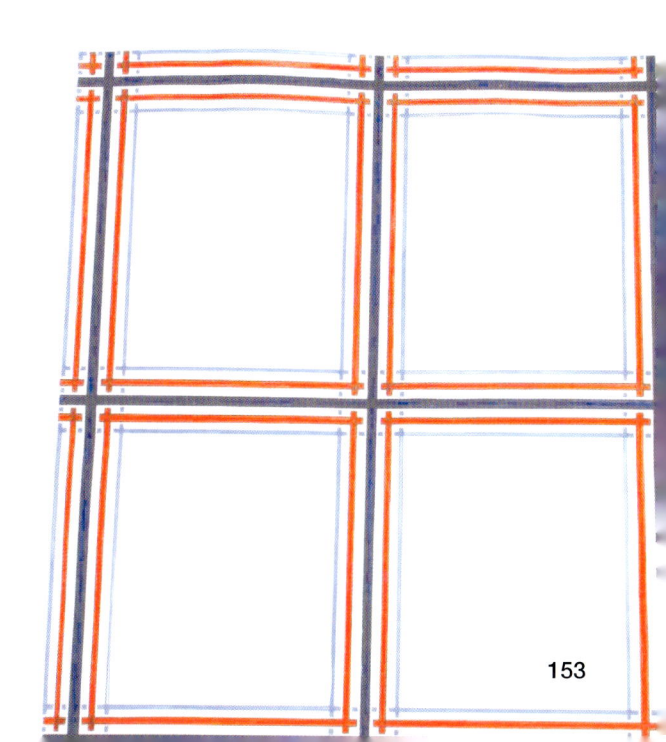

The Percy Bass Decorator's Guide

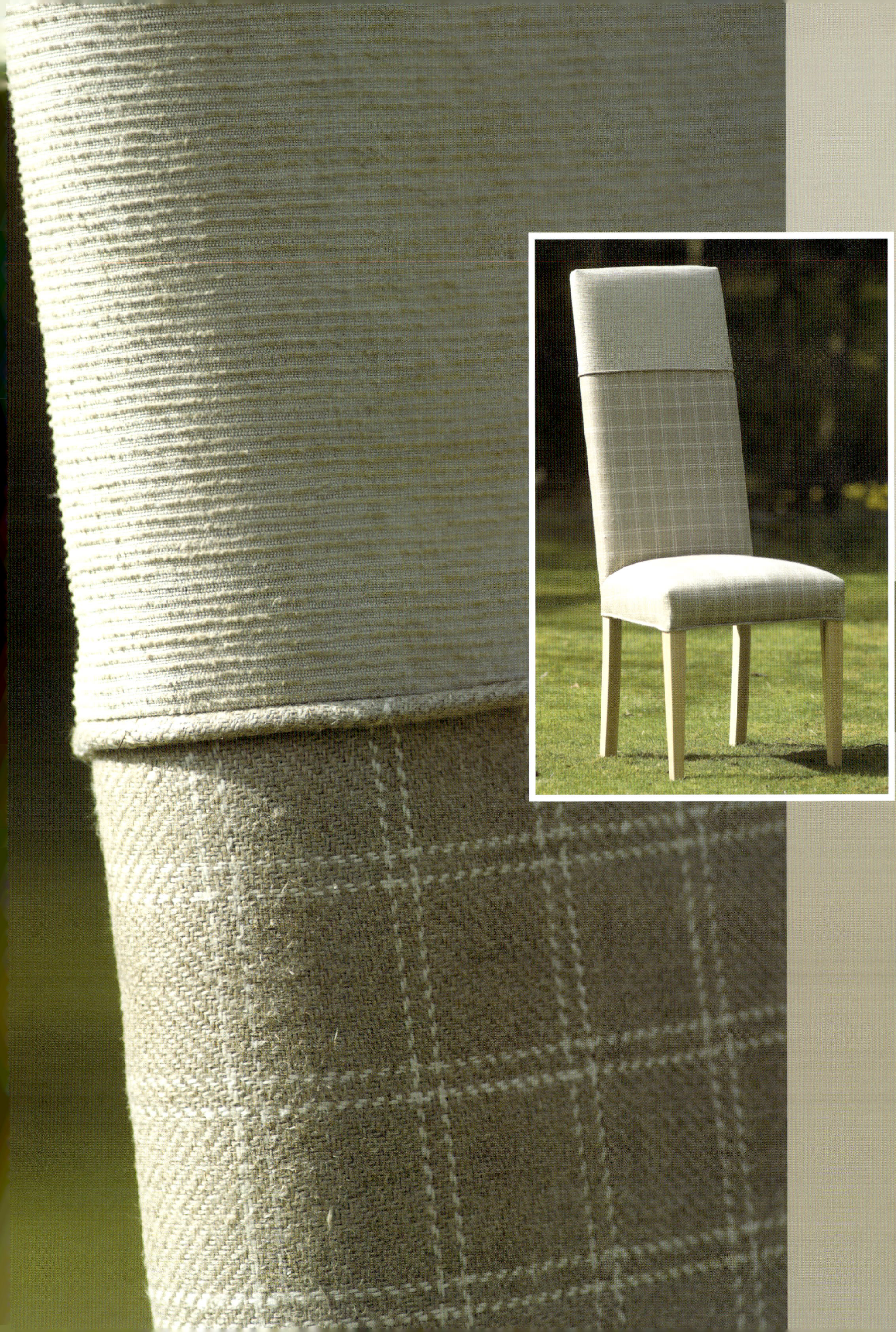

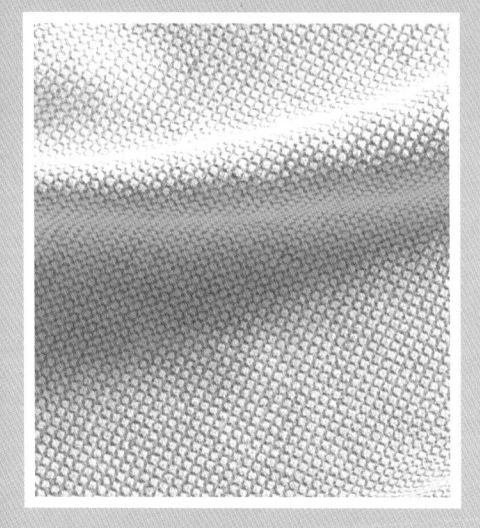

Naturals, a collection of heavy weight and textured cottons and linens

Classic English style is what characterises the fabrics for this long-established company. High-quality furnishing fabrics, both printed and woven, are designed to suit both traditional and contemporary interiors.

Titley and Marr

Originally, Titley and Marr produced printed fabrics inspired by the rich traditions of English nineteenth-century woodblock printed designs. As time has passed the style of design has changed. Retaining inspiration from traditional documents, the designers have altered the scale and colourations to suit modern-day living environments. Fabrics made of textured yarns, wools, linen and cotton, combined with a mix of natural colours and rich vibrant hues, predominate the collection.

The company has always prided itself in manufacturing almost all of its products in the UK. Only when specialist techniques are required is its production moved to mills in Europe.

Recent collections include Balmoral and Sandringham, a traditional cotton damask with a coordinating stripe woven in 14 diverse colours from the palest chalk white to dramatic maroon, aubergine and the richest reds. Naturals is a collection of cottons and linens, heavyweight and textured, suitable for curtains and upholstery with a flame-proof finish to suit all situations. Cube and Linear is a range of contemporary taffeta fabrics with an interesting highlight of chenille. Strong dramatic colours and natural earth tones provide a broad colour palette. Broadway Velvet, the most recent addition to the collection, is a viscose velvet with a narrow stripe and antique finish. Colours in this fabric include opulent theatrical reds, greens, and browns through to palest sandstone and cream.

Contact Details

Titley and Marr Ltd
Unit B4 Hazleton Estate
Horndean
Hampshire PO8 9JU
Tel: 023 9259 9585

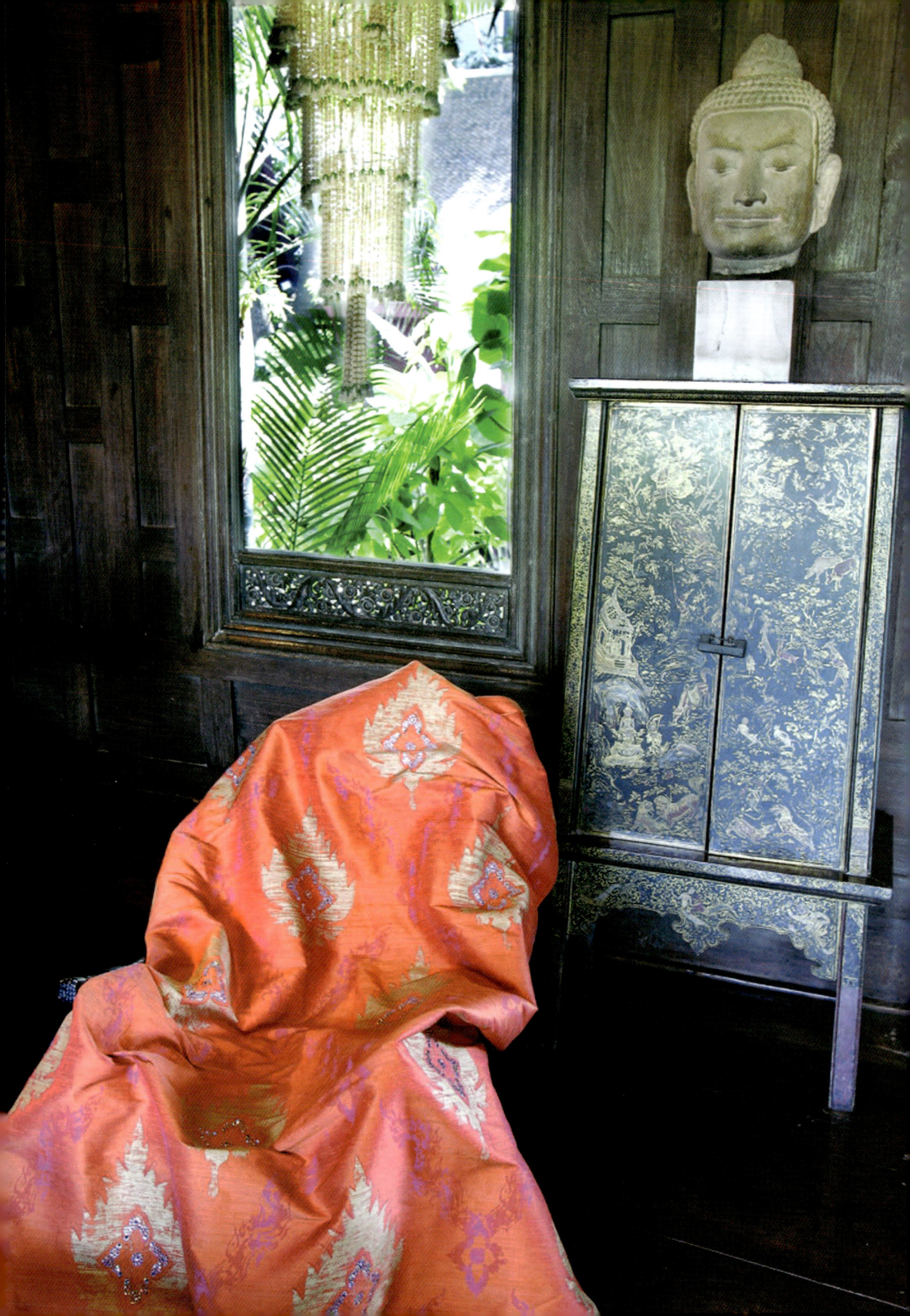

Opposite: Fan Club 11 from the Crystal collection; Left: Jim Thompson; Below: Venus from the Deities collection

Jim Thompson

This legendary American set foot in Bangkok in the 1940s and created a lasting reputation for glorious Thai silks of the highest quality. Today the company has updated collections that are imbued with a luxurious mix of colours, textures and warmth.

For over half a century Jim Thompson has been known as the legendary manufacturer of Thai silk. Through the company's respect for the history of textiles, and its profound knowledge of traditional and modern techniques, the name Jim Thompson remains today synonymous with Thai silk of highest quality and design. As much care and attention is given to traditionally hand-dyed and hand-woven textiles as to fabrics created from advanced precision power looms. The result is a most complete fabric collection for the home, suitable for domestic and contract use in both contemporary and traditional interiors.

By the late 1940s, when Jim Thompson arrived in Thailand from the USA, the availability of cheap machine-made fabrics from abroad meant that the production of hand-woven silk was becoming a dying trade. Jim Thompson became involved in silk weaving through local villagers in the vicinity of his Bangkok home and by combining western influences such as replacing the traditional vegetable dyes with colourfast European dyes, he placed Thailand back on the map for these glorious silks we see today. His talent as a colourist ensured that Jim Thompson fabrics were used all over the world – from Hollywood film sets to Windsor Castle.

Contemporary collections

Today, Jim Thompson brings out two new collections a year. The Autumn/Spring collection uses innovation in design and weaving techniques to create a collection of luxurious silks woven on the hand and Jacquard looms, silk/cotton mixes and linens which are characterised by textures and dimension, as well as a long-lasting durability.

Jim Thompson's fabric collections for the interior, updated every season, are a sensual mix of colours, textures and warmth. A strong sensitivity and attention to detail flows through every design. There is harmony within each collection, and at the same time abundant individuality. Jim Thompson's silks are much admired by interior designers both at home and abroad.

Contact Details

Jim Thompson
2/9 Fox Linton
Chelsea Harbour Design Centre
London
SW10 0XE
Tel: 020 7368 7700
Fax: 020 7368 7701
Email: info@foxlinton.com
Website: www.jimthompson.com

The Percy Bass Decorator's Guide

Having worked closely with several high-profile fabric companies, including Colefax and Fowler and Charles Hammond of Sloane Street, Bernard Thorp started his own fabric design business in 1971. The business has grown steadily over the years, enjoying increasing demand, with commissions from both the UK and overseas. Bernard Thorp & Co Ltd now has dedicated showrooms in London and Paris and an extensive network of distributors worldwide.

With its main showrooms located in Chelsea, the epicentre for the capital's most prestigious furnishing outlets, the business has acquired an enviable reputation for supplying the finest commissioned furnishing fabrics.

Above, from left:
Knightsbridge on Suede;
Kensington Flower

Bernard Thorp & Co Ltd

Founded by Bernard Thorp in the early 1970s, Chelsea-based Bernard Thorp & Co Ltd is now considered one of Europe's leading designers and manufacturers of bespoke furnishing fabrics and wall coverings.

Left: Wisley cotton;
Below: Kensington, Wrought and Fougere

As a design-led company, Bernard Thorp & Co Ltd is committed to producing the finest range of furnishing fabrics and customised wallpapers. All fabrics are created to suit each client's particular requirements and personal tastes. Its London and Paris showrooms hold an incredible library of fabrics, including numerous historical patterns alongside more contemporary designs, which act as a source of inspiration for many interior designers.

The design and print production of the fabrics takes place at the London factory showrooms, with the woven fabrics produced in Suffolk and the wallpapers in Norfolk. Bernard Thorp takes great pride in producing its fabrics exclusively in the UK.

Commissions continue to increase, with a high percentage of repeat business generated from satisfied clients and leading interior designers. With extensive experience of the interior design industry and an ability to create truly individual designs, Bernard Thorp is often involved in the transformation of high-profile corporate and theatrical establishments, restaurants and hotels, as well as numerous prestigious residential projects.

With all specially made fabrics being created to suit individual clients' specifications, Bernard Thorp takes a very flexible approach to its manufacturing and is able to accommodate unusual requests such as small fabric quantities or urgent commissions (sometimes within 24 hours).

Innovative and imaginative, with a dedication to producing the highest-quality bespoke fabrics, Bernard Thorp continues to achieve exceptional standards of design, quality and service, both in the UK and internationally.

Contact Details

Bernard Thorp & Co Ltd
Tel: 020 7352 5745
Email: info@bernardthorp.com
Website: www.bernardthorp.com

London showroom
53 Chelsea Manor Street
London SW3 5RZ
UK
Tel: 020 7352 5745/5457/1022
Fax: 020 7376 3640

New York showroom
Old World Weavers at Stark Carpets
D&D Building
979 Third Avenue, 10th Floor
NY 10022
USA
Tel: +1 212 355 7186
Fax: +1 212 593 0761

Paris showroom
10 Avenue de Villars
75007 Paris
France
Tel: +33 1 4753 7637
Fax: +33 1 4555 9781

Contact Details

Today Interiors Ltd
Hollis Road
Grantham
Lincolnshire
NG31 7QH
Tel: 01476 574401
Fax: 01476 590208
Email: info@today-interiors.co.uk
Website: www.today-interiors.com

FR4474 Cercle curtain;
Inset: FR4470 Cercle curtain,
FR4452 Opera cushion,
FR4461 Smoke cushion (from
the new Farandole collection);
Bottom: Medici & Galleria

Today Interiors

Influenced by constantly changing design trends, including texture and colour, this well-established company continues to be innovative in design and meet customers' requirements, be they commercial or private specifications.

Established for over 30 years, Today Interiors is best known as a major supplier of fabrics and wall coverings to the hotel industry, the contract market and to the professional interior designer. It is these markets that insist on innovative design that meets all the exacting technical specifications required for the project. Today Interiors' reputation is based on meeting these standards supported by an ex-stock service and delivery excellence.

Today Interiors collections are available from all major and leading specialist retail outlets throughout the UK.

In March 2005 Today Interiors joined forces with Natasha Marshall and Squigee on a licensing agreement to exclusively distribute the Natasha Marshall collections of fabrics and wall coverings worldwide.

Extensive stocks are held in the UK for immediate despatch. Prices range from, £21 to £47 excluding VAT.

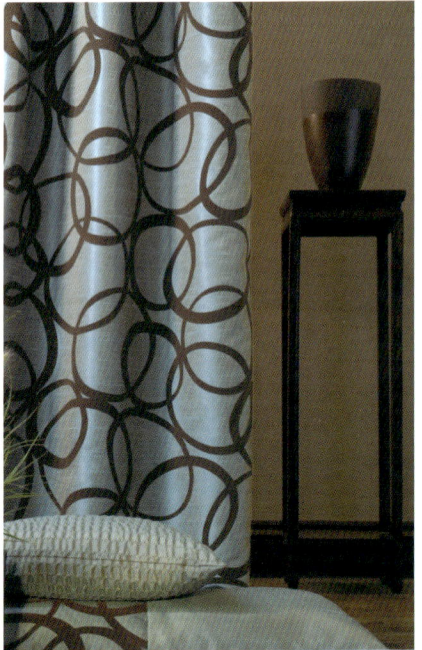

Trimmings By Design

For over 100 years, this company has supplied decorative trimmings to the interior decorating and furnishing markets, safe in the knowledge that its traditional skills will be preserved from generation to generation.

Trimmings By Design has evolved through its wealth of experience and technological expertise to become the UK's largest decorative trimmings manufacturer, sustaining a distinguished worldwide reputation for its high-quality products, service and design creativity.

The company's interdependent relationship between old and new methods enables traditional machinery to be used in conjunction with new electronic technology, creating woven braids, twisted cords, knitted fringes and handmade tassels in a most efficient and effective way, without compromising the design and quality of the finished product.

No interior design scheme is complete without the attention to detail that passementerie provides, adding a professional edge to create a truly unique look. Working with the company's design studio, customers can create a fresh and exciting personal collection of bespoke passementerie, offering maximum freedom of choice and selection.

From opulent palaces to chic contemporary apartments, the flexibility of craftsmanship continually realises clients' own concepts. This is complemented by a vast range of colours in the highest quality yarns from pure linen, cottons and rayons to silks, custom-dyed if required to match precisely to clients' fabrics.

The extensive archive library dating back to the early 1800s is an important source of inspiration, whether creating a bespoke trimming or an exclusive passementerie collection. Whatever the style, passementerie is a prerequisite of all decorating schemes from the simplest of fine cords to the Baroque extravagance of an embellished fringe.

Trimmings By Design Ltd is a trade-only company.

Avebury single tassel tieback, together with cord and gimp rosette

The design studio will work with clients to create bespoke passementerie, colour-matched precisely to their fabrics

Contact Details

Trimmings By Design Ltd
Gresham Road
Derby
DE24 8AW
Tel: 01332 331314
Fax: 01332 292977
Email: enquiry@trimmingsbydesign.co.uk

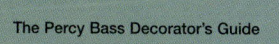

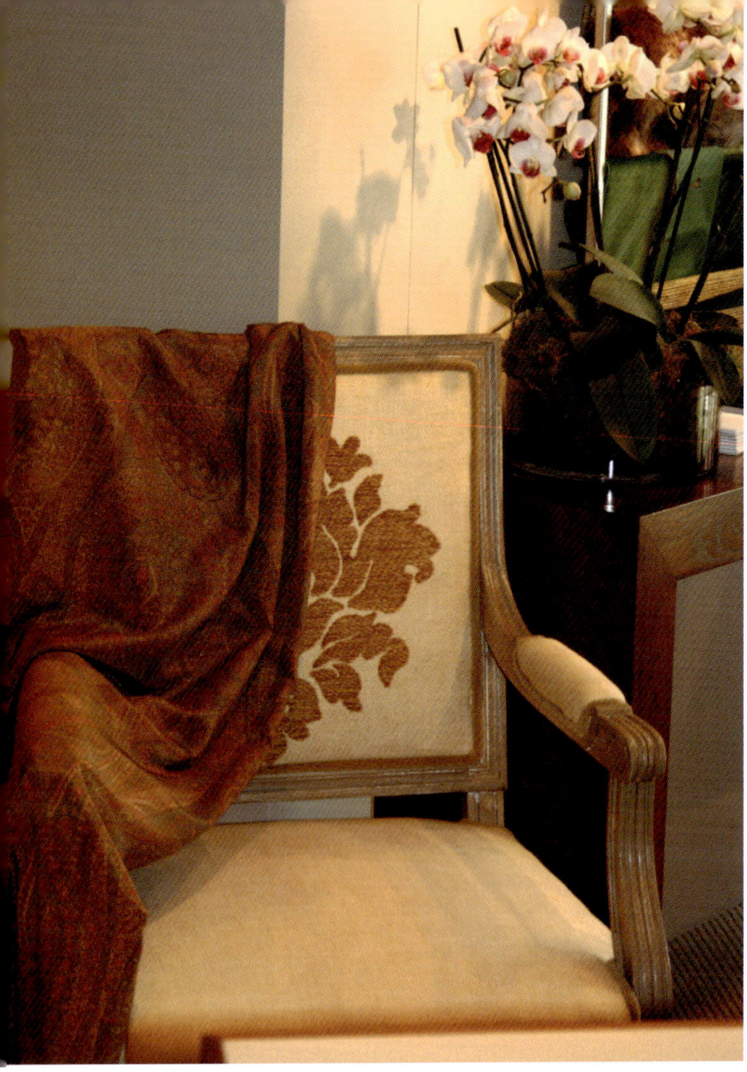
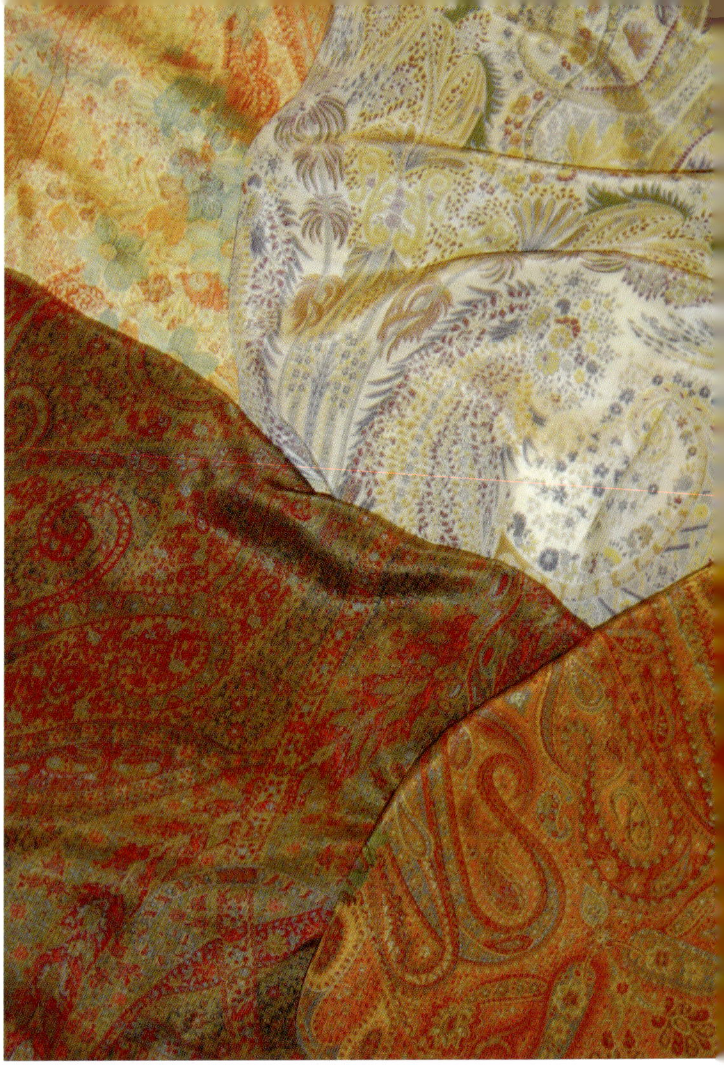
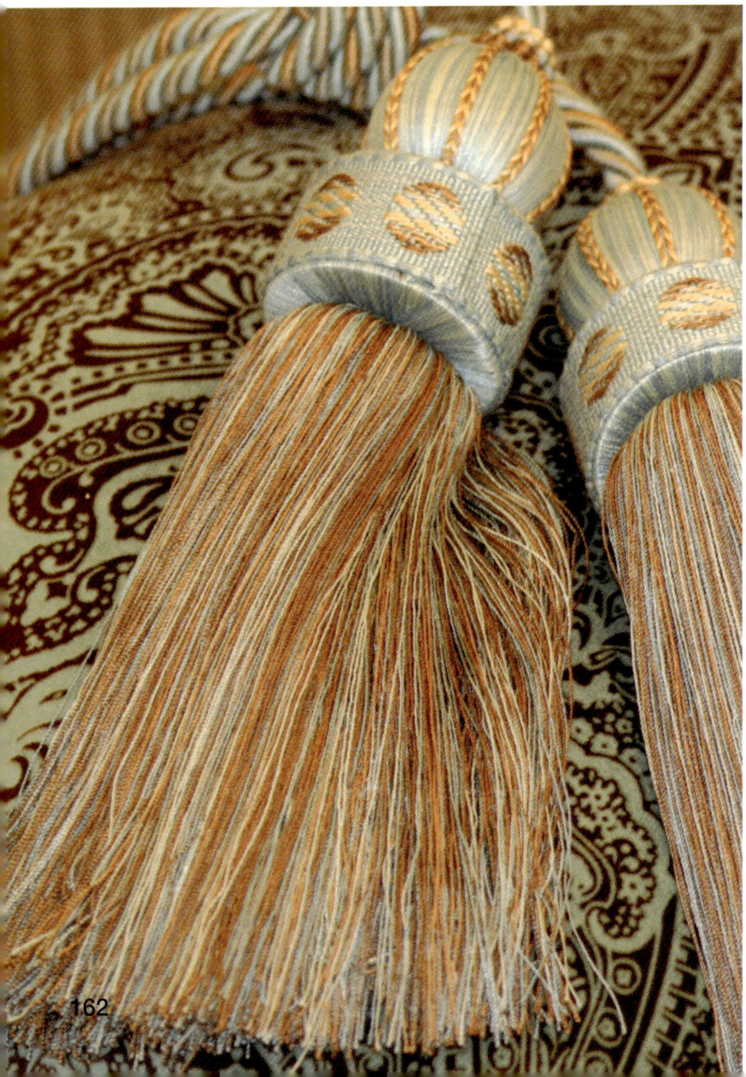
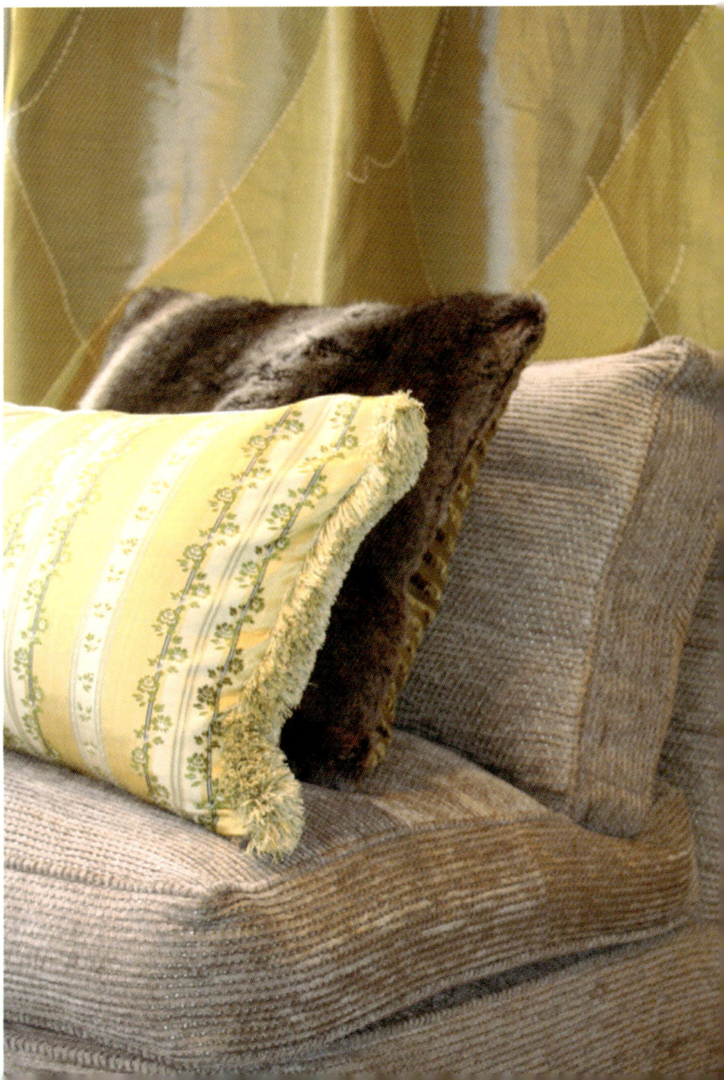

Opposite, clockwise from top left: Chair, Decortex Gaeta DX1958/3, throw, Nepal Crepe Col1, Voghi; selection of Paisleys from Voghi; chair, Kligi Kenzan 4024/6, back cushion, Voghi Matarol Col2, front cushion, Edmond Petit Longueville PET 13377, curtain Decortex Veronesi DX2141/3; Graziana-Schumacher cushion 171004, tie back from Les Passementeries de L'Ile de France

Turnell & Gigon Distribution

Founded in 1985, this is the original company in the group, which distributes the finest fabrics and trimmings from around the world.

A wide range of contemporary and traditional companies are represented by Turnell & Gigon Distribution, including:

- Burger, Paris
- Cesari, Rome
- Decortex, Florence
- Greeff, USA
- Hamot, France
- Les Passementeries de L'Ile de France, Paris
- Kligi, Venice
- Edmond Petit, Paris
- Schumacher, USA
- S.A.T. Creations, Paris
- Veraseta, Paris
- Voghi, Como

Designer collection

Charles Burger is renowned for its stunning eighteenth-century toile de Jouy designs and beautiful historical prints.

Together with a wonderful collection of traditional brocades and damasks, Cesari also has a range of contemporary plains and textures.

Specialising in striking contemporary innovative weaves, Decortex designs include everything from bold patterns to textured plains.

A wonderful collection of prints and weaves in the American tradition is produced by Greeff.

Kligi has innovative products manufactured with the best possible yarns and the most up-to-date techniques.

One of the largest collections of tiebacks, tassels, ropes, rosettes and cords, Les Passementeries de L'ile de France trimmings are available in many colours and styles, contemporary or traditional.

A wealth of historical prints and weaves comes from Edmond Petit/Hamot, together with a large range of velvets and other textures, all woven in the classic French tradition.

S.A.T. Creations are versatile weaves including an impressive collection of faux suede and crushed velvets.

A prolific collection of glamorous prints and weaves come from Schumacher, a truly international house.

Veraseta offers an extensive range of the highest quality silk taffetas, satins and silk weaves.

Voghi collections include beautiful printed paisleys on different qualities, wonderful damasks and a large selection of faux furs.

Decortex Dune DX2139/1

Contact Details

Turnell & Gigon Distribution
Chelsea Harbour Design Centre
Lots Road
London
SW10 0XE
Tel: 020 8971 1711
Fax: 020 8971 1716
Email: sales@turnellandgigon.com
Website: www.tandggroup.com

Vervain comprises over 160 patterned printed and woven fabrics. Available at S.Harris/Fabricut showrooms and selected high-end showrooms across the country, Vervain's fabrics are inspired by documentary textiles and original, classic designs.

Vervain, a distinctive new brand of textiles, was introduced into the high-end interior design marketplace in the spring of 2004. Created with romance, beauty and vibrancy in mind, Vervain will set a new standard for traditional design.

Vervain

Opposite and right: Manchuria Clover, width 142cm, repeat 95cm, 100 per cent cotton, three colours; Inset: Satsuma artwork, width 137cm, 100 per cent cotton, four colours; Below: Porcellana Black, width 140cm, repeat 72cm, 86 per cent cotton, 8 per cent nylon and 6 per cent polyester, two colours

'We sought to create a high-end traditional line, and we are thrilled with the result of Vervain,' says Vervain vice president David Klaristenfeld. 'While firmly rooted in the traditional style, Vervain's breadth of patterns and colour selection will create a dynamic statement. Vervain is a beautifully diverse line that will work well in any classic interior.'

Timeless prints
Stylistically, the print designs include documentary florals, vibrant Chinoiseries, damasks and toiles. Printed on elegant ground cloths and carefully manufactured to highlight fine detail and distinctive colour combinations, Vervain offers an exciting new resource for traditional prints.

Weaving the past into the future
The Vervain woven collection includes damasks, velvets, Jacquards, brocades and tapestries. The highest quality is obtained through the combination of intricate weaving and a wide range of yarns and fibres, predominantly cotton, linen and silk.

'When designing the woven collection, we were inspired by centuries-old fabrics, and we created original woven designs based on prints and paintings,' says Nina Butkin, vice president of design. 'Vervain's woven colour palette reflects both our print collection and the foremost interior style of design.'

Vervain patterns are the culmination of extensive research and development. Uniting the history and aura of documentary fabrics with new classic designs, Vervain defines textiles of artistry and distinction.

Contact Details

Vervain
Distributed by Alton-Brooke
2–25 Chelsea Harbour Design Centre
Lots Road, London SW10 0XE
Tel: 020 7376 7008
Fax: 020 7376 7009
Email: info@alton-brooke.co.uk
Website: www.alton-brooke.co.uk

The Percy Bass Decorator's Guide

Offering luxury fabrics that inspire and surpass consumer expectations, Voyage Decoration sources an eclectic range of exclusive fabrics from around the world. The product selection is vast, featuring over 2500 designs which make up over 40 collections, including chenilles, crewels, silks, Jacquards, damasks, linens and handmade fabrics.

Voyage Decoration

Voyage believes that fabric for children's rooms should be fun and has a wonderful range of colourful, handmade fabrics embellished with appliqué, embroidery and buttons. Themes include boats, teddy bears, fairies, rockets and cars.

Beautiful Italian Jacquards influenced by ancient Turkish textile designs make up the Topkapi range. Fabric from this collection would give a rich eastern feel to any room.

Voyage's crewel fabrics are hand-stitched with pure wool in Kashmir by home-based artisans. Highly decorative, these fabrics truly are pieces of art.

Eastern-inspired silks are embroidered with silk thread, beading and jewelled fabrics. These are some of the collection's most luxurious fabrics, with colours ranging from deep, rich colours to pale, elegant shades.

Modern, city styles are reflected in the Trapani, Electra, Orpheus and Horizon collections. All are completely different but seriously stylish.

Contact Details

Voyage Decoration Ltd
Unit 1 Block 4
39 Clydesmill Place
Clydesmill Industrial Estate
Glasgow
G32 8RF
Tel: 0141 641 1700
Fax: 0141 643 3430
Email: info@voyfab.co.uk
Website: www.voyagedecoration.com

WarnerFabrics

With a well-established history, this company today enjoys a preference for prints and weaves in the UK and chintzes and wallpapers in the USA. However, it is still a proud holder of the Royal Warrant.

Left: Twiggy Bird
Below: Anastasia

Benjamin Warner founded his silk weaving firm on 23 November 1869. Warner & Sons established itself in Spitalfields, east London and quickly secured a reputation for producing high quality silks, becoming the foremost furnishing silk weaver in the UK. In 1874 the firm began supplying bespoke chintz fabrics to complement the silk weaving.

Success meant that it outgrew its premises in Spitalfields and moved to the site of New Mills in Braintree, Essex in 1895. Here it continued to weave silk, damask, brocades, brocatelles and velvets.

English Heritage
Warner & Sons began supplying the Royal Household with commissioned silk in 1871. From generation to generation, the firm weaved silk and velvet for every English coronation, beginning with that of Edward VII in 1902. The coronation of Queen Elizabeth in 1953 saw the firm weaving most of the fabrics.

While somewhere along the way the name has been changed from Warner & Sons to Warner Fabrics, the essence of the company remains the same.

The quintessentially English image associated with Warner is still very much alive and a part of the company continues to produce old classics. Hampton, its earliest print, and Portuguese Tapestry, its oldest design, are both current.

Recent collections include:
- Hortus – bold large-scale florals with co-ordinating weaves.
- Ebury – a stunning damask weave in 40 colours.
- Sheer Indulgence – a collection of sheers, voiles and laces.
- Miniatures and Complements – useful small-scale wallpapers and prints.

Contact Details

Warner Fabrics
T & G Group of Companies
Chelsea Harbour Design Centre
Lots Road
London
SW10 0XE
Tel: 020 8971 1713
Fax: 020 8971 1716
Email: sales@warnerfabrics.com
Website: www.warnerfabrics.com

Chair Victorian Star, cushion Maryport

Above: Manhattan Collection: Sofa – Elegance Mink, Chair – Uno Topaz, Ottoman – Luminous Topaz, Cushions (clockwise) Loop Turquoise, Elegance Mink, Luminous Turquoise, Velveteen Malachite, Oracle Opal; Right, from top: Aria Topaz, Oracle Opal, Aria Topaz; Below: Manhattan stacking cushions, from top: Orion Truffle, Snap Onyx, Aria Onyx, Luminous Quartz, Mien Onyx

With the backing of its powerful Australian parent company, Warwick Fabrics (UK) Ltd is flourishing in its role as a creator of soft furnishing fabrics for the worldwide residential market and as a promoter of classic British linen florals. Its fabrics can be found in first-class hotel chains and also grace the residences of many state leaders.

Warwick Fabrics

Set up in the mid 1980s in the heart of the Cotswolds, Warwick Fabrics (UK) Ltd is part of the Warwick Group of Companies, founded in Australia 40 years ago by brothers Tom and Max Warwick. Now one of the most successful privately owned textile groups worldwide, with an annual turnover exceeding €40m, the group orchestrates its sales through two main operating hubs: Warwick Australia & New Zealand, covering Australasia and the Far East, and Warwick UK, distributing soft furnishing fabrics throughout Europe, the Americas, Africa and the Middle East.

In 1993, Warwick Fabrics (UK) Ltd was awarded the highly coveted Queens Award for Export Achievement, in recognition of its contribution to exports. Warwick now exports to over 50 countries.

British classics
Warwick has done much over the past 20 years to promote and enhance the reputation of classic British vat-printed linen florals, driven from its unique in-house colour studio in Manchester, and backed up by its design studio in Italy, reflecting the international flavour of the company. Warwick also offers an impressive range of transitional and contemporary fabric collections.

Contract successes
With many of its ranges stocked FR-treated and meeting high specifications, in recent years the world's leading hospitality specifiers have selected Warwick fabrics for the bedrooms and public spaces of many hotel chains including Le Meridian and the Sheraton. A recent high-profile contract at the beginning of 2004 involved supplying the Marriott West India Quay in London with 3000m of silk.

The current Warwick collections can be viewed through the group website at www.warwick.com.au. Further information on the Warwick collections and details of distributors and agents worldwide is available from the head office in Bourton-on-the-Water.

Clockwise, from above: Mayfair Collection – Citrus – Chair Meribelle Orchid, Scatter Cushions Vasette Citrus, Meribelle Lilac; Mayfair Citrus – Doona Cover Pixie Cirus, Vasette Citrus Pillow Cases Vasette Citrus, Olivia Citrus; Mayfair Raindrop – Chair Floral Vasette Blush, Chair Striped Elsie Raindrop, Scatter Cushions Polkadot Raindrop, Floret Blush, Pixie Raindrop, Mayfair Raindrop, Day Bed Cushions Mayfair Raindrop, Pixie Raindrop, Drop Eve Blush; Mayfair Citrus Elsie Citrus, Polkadot Raindrop, Floret Coral, Vasette Citrus; Mayfair Sky – Scatter Cushions Polkadot Sky, Elsie Sky, Bag Vasette Sky, Elsie Sky

Contact Details

Warwick Fabrics Ltd
Hackling House
Bourton Industrial Park
Bourton-on-the-Water
Gloucestershire
GL54 2HQ
Tel: 01451 822383
Fax: 01451 822369
Email: info@warwick.co.uk
Website: www.warwick.co.uk

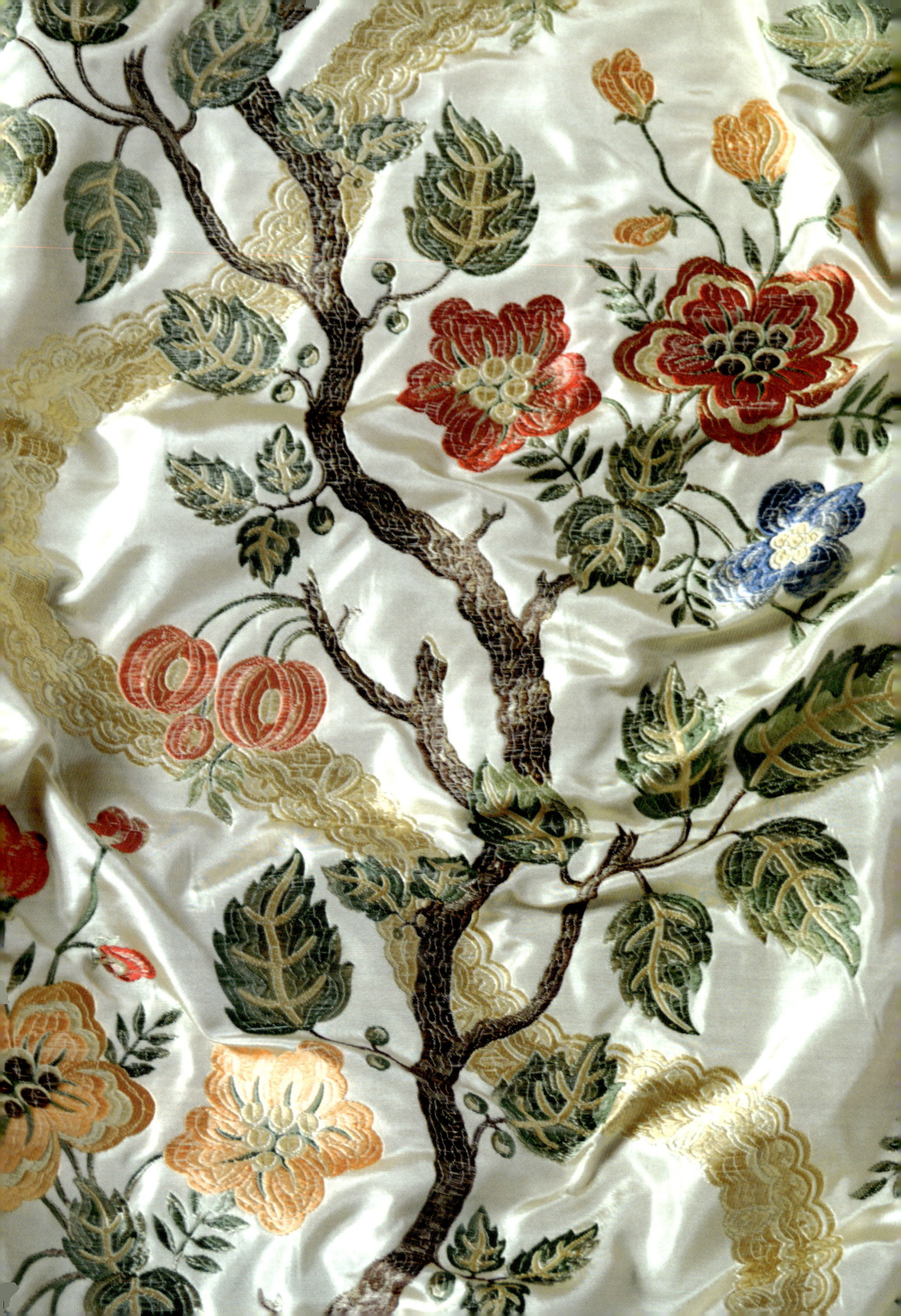

An individual with eclectic sense, George Gilbert Scott not only designed the red telephone box and the Albert Memorial but also founded a company that continues to this day to stir up romantic, decorative dreams.

Watts of Westminster's London showroom, at Chelsea Harbour Design Centre, is a magnet for those searching for something real and different in a design world that increasingly feels the same. Founded in 1874 by George Gilbert Scott – designer of the red telephone box, the Albert Memorial and Battersea Power Station – Watts maintains an individual, eclectic design ethic, which in 2005 has become the antidote to the neutral design palette of the last decade. Huge, glorious late nineteenth-century patterns are a refreshing alternative to the late twentieth-century aversion to scale. An exuberance of colour invades the senses and becomes the stuff of rich, romantic, decorative dreams – an escape from the habitual bland tones of grey-suited uniformity.

Swathes of glorious silk damask, the richest brocatelles, velvets and chunky chenilles inspire and excite, wallpapers decorate rather than whisper, and passementerie is a cornucopia of jewel-like baubles rather than a formal collection.

Palatial opulence

Pattern, historically, is global; people have always travelled. Watts, a unique English company with a powerful archive of genuine design, reflects a growing trend towards supply beyond the constraints of the English vernacular. Versatility in production has helped realise designs inspired by A.W.N. Pugin – who designed the interiors of the palaces of Westminster – at Prestonfield, Edinburgh's super-opulent celebrity hideaway hotel, and the ultimate in luxury, the seven-star Burj Al Arab Hotel in Dubai.

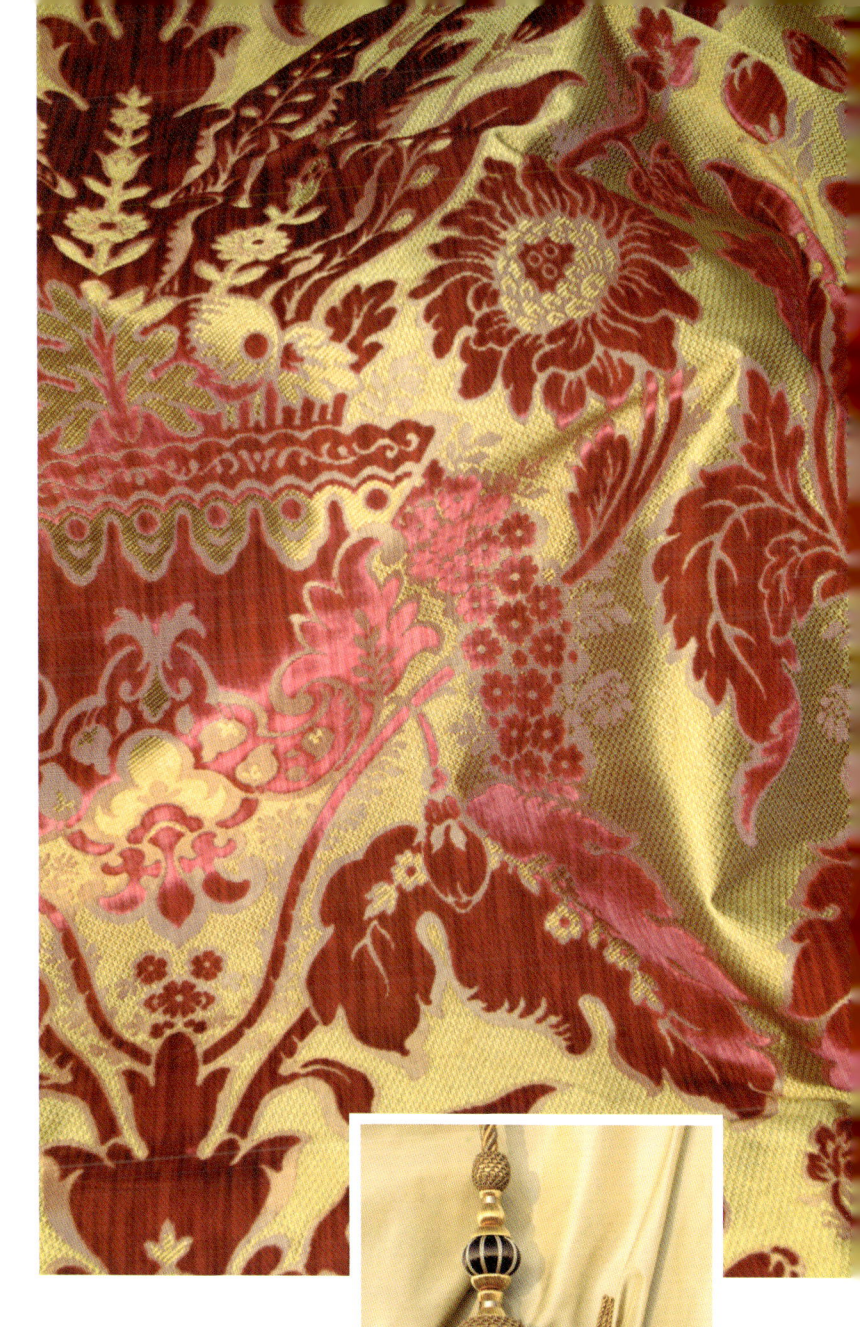

Opposite: Haddon Asquith Cream, silk; Above: Versailles Rose Gold, silk cut velvet; Inset: Besancon Passementerie tassel tieback

Watts
of Westminster

Contact Details

Watts of Westminster
Chelsea Harbour Design Centre
London
SW10 0XE
UK
Tel: 020 7376 4486
Fax: 020 7376 4636
Email: sales@wattsofwestminster.com
Website: www.wattsofwestminster.com

Also represented in the showroom:
Belinda Coote
Jackson & Co

Above: Marquis/Creme, an exuberant printed silk from Johannes Wellmann;
Below: Losone/Ecru, linen with embroidery; Ascona/Ecru, wool mix tartan;
Odessa/Citrine tasselled tieback with bronze top from Henry Newbery

Johannes Wellmann Fabrics

This highly regarded textile editor combines traditional and contemporary design elements in stylish and original fabrics of the highest quality.

Henry Newbery enjoys exclusive distribution rights for Johannes Wellman fabrics in the UK and Irish Republic. These exquisite textiles are displayed at the Newbery London West End showroom, where plains, patterns, sheers, prints, weaves and embroideries jostle for attention.

Johannes Wellmann founded his textile editing business in 1919 in the historic city of Cologne, the largest city in North-Rhine Westphalia and a vibrant centre of art and commerce. The company has expanded greatly since its foundation and is today run by the charismatic managing partners, Johannes and Christophe Wellmann.

Central to its operation are offices and warehouses in Cologne and prestigious showrooms in Paris and Antwerp. Further showrooms in major cities around the world, together with a comprehensive distribution and agent network, ensure that the brand is highly regarded in both the domestic and contract furnishing markets.

Using a wide variety of high-quality yarns and state-of-the-art weaving techniques, the collections offer excitingly textured surfaces and luminous colours. Wellmann's in-house designers, inspired by classical design and contemporary trends, create stunningly original textiles. Efficient service, attention to detail and quality control are hallmarks of the marque, and practicality is definitely not sacrificed at the altar of aesthetics. The curtain fabrics drape beautifully and upholstery cloths offer high abrasion-resistance and durability. An effective backup of generous stock levels with rapid sampling and delivery provide an absolutely first class service to designers and furnishers all over the world.

Fired by enthusiasm for these gorgeous fabrics, Newbery sales director Clem Malone and his team are proud to offer the Wellmann range as a stylish compliment to the Newbery trimmings collections. In the ever-changing world of interior fashion, Johannes Wellmann remains one of Europe's most prestigious textile editors, offering a wonderfully stylish blend of tradition and modernity to the discerning end user.

Above: Theben & Sparta, supple and robust upholstery cloths from Johannes Wellmann

Contact Details

Johannes Wellmann Fabrics
Distributed by Henry Newbery & Co. Ltd.
18 Newman Street
London W1T 1AB
Trade contact details
Pauline Ellis
Clem Malone
Tel: 020 7636 5970
Fax: 020 7436 6406
Email: sales@henrynewbery.com
Websites: www.henrynewbery.com
www.wellmann.net

The Percy Bass Decorator's Guide

Silk has been woven in the same idyllic Georgian Whitchurch Silk Mill since 1820. The 1815 clock installed to celebrate the victory at Waterloo remains, as does the pounding waterwheel which operates a winding machine. The Mill is a time capsule which produces the finest quality silks for customers who are keen to have a fabric that exactly satisfies their requirements.

Whitchurch Silk Mill is proud to have woven silk for numerous interiors, for stage and screen productions, a number of public commissions, such as banners for a hospital and the Great Hall in Winchester, and commissions for Cathedrals.

The design team is well practised at interpreting a customer's concepts or devising completely fresh ideas. Customers may choose to be involved in developing a design and may even wish to see their fabric being woven. All of this is welcomed.

The Mill weaves plain or striped silks in any colourway. All yarn is dyed to match. Typically warps are silk, but a range of yarns including silk are used in the weft, as required. Commonly Whitchurch weaves taffetas, organzas, Ottomans and twills, which are used for curtains, blinds, walls, bed hangings and light upholstery.

Whitchurch's weavers can even weave as little as 25 metres and as much as you want. Fabrics can be supplied directly from the loom or printed, and can be moiréd and softened. Prices are dependent on the length of your order and the number of colours in the design. Prices start at approximately £80 per metre for a 25 metre order and decrease to approximately £43 per metre for larger orders.

If uniqueness, authenticity and keeping alive our British heritage are important, then visit Whitchurch Silk Mill – a charity determined to maintain its attention to detail in bringing customers wonderful silks with a flexible service.

Whitchurch Silk Mill

Whitchurch Silk Mill weaves silk on Victorian looms using traditional skills to recreate the best of the past – and some pretty exciting contemporary fabrics.

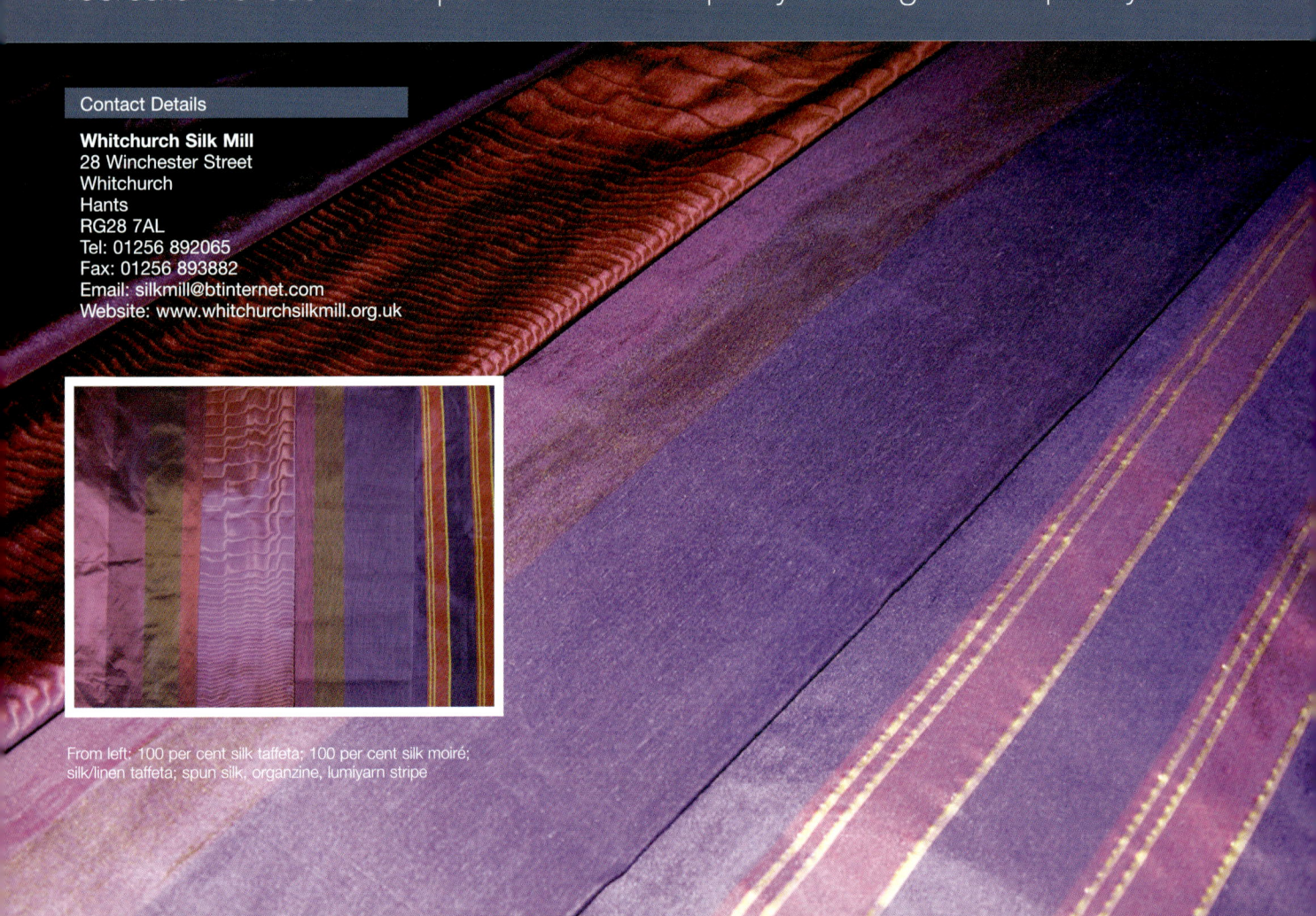

Contact Details

Whitchurch Silk Mill
28 Winchester Street
Whitchurch
Hants
RG28 7AL
Tel: 01256 892065
Fax: 01256 893882
Email: silkmill@btinternet.com
Website: www.whitchurchsilkmill.org.uk

From left: 100 per cent silk taffeta; 100 per cent silk moiré; silk/linen taffeta; spun silk; organzine, lumiyarn stripe

Fran White

Bolts of linen in the shop

Simplicity and natural elegance characterise the linen and linen blend fabrics on offer from this company. They are ideal for curtains, cushions and bedding, and are subtle enough for both modern and traditional settings.

Fran White Woven Textiles and The Linen Shop design, manufacture and distribute a range of linen and linen blend fabrics. These fabrics are designed by Fran White and are woven in Ireland, the UK and Belgium. Retail prices are between £15 and £47 per metre. The company deals with customers throughout the UK, Europe, the Middle East, Australia and North America.

The Linen Shop is stocked from floor to ceiling with bolts of Fran's linen designs. They vary in weight and texture and are suitable for curtains, as they hang and drape so well. As cushions, bedding, light upholstery and table linen, the fabrics add a little natural elegance to any interior space. Their understated simplicity provides a subtle and tranquil background for use in both modern and more traditional settings.

Fabrics and clothing

The company's catalogue shows the range of fabrics currently stocked, as well as the simple collection of Linen Wearables (clothing pieces). Everything in the catalogue is available by mail order. Customers can visit the shop to find further designs and special offers, remnants, quilting kits, handmade scarves, bags and cushions.

A swatch and returnable samples service is offered. Testing a fabric in your home with furniture and décor is something that is encouraged, as lighting will always differ.

The company works closely with its customers and mills to maintain excellent quality control. As a consequence, lead times on larger orders can occasionally stretch from three months to a year!

Contact Details

Fran White Woven Textiles
The Linen Shop
Cooks Farm
Nuthurst
Horsham
West Sussex
RH13 6LH
Tel: 01403 891073
Fax: 01403 891371
Email: fabric@franwhite.com
Website: www.franwhite.com

178

The Percy Bass Decorator's Guide

SHEILA COOMBES
Opposite, clockwise from top left:
Free Spirit, Woven Wind 02;
Free Spirit, Moonshine 01;
New Botanicals, Butterfly Ball 3085-02;
Free Spirit, Eastern Promise 02

Brian Yates offers one of the most comprehensive selections of wall coverings and fabrics on the market. Innovation, good styling and quality are at the forefront of the philosophy of the company.

Brian Yates

Brian Yates was established over 25 years ago by managing director Brian Yates and design director Sheila Coombes.

The sales office located near Lancaster at the southern tip of the South Lake District gives friendly, efficient help with orders, despatch, and technical information. This is supported by a speedy warehousing facility with personnel who can despatch orders and samples within 24 hours.

The Brian Yates trade showroom is located in the prestigious Chelsea Harbour Design Centre, where all the wallcoverings and fabrics can be viewed in a user-friendly environment.

As well as representing some of the most forward-thinking design companies, Brian Yates sells and markets the triple award-winning Sheila Coombes brand of exclusive fabrics and wallpapers. These include printed linens and cottons, unusual weaves, velvets, chenilles wool and silks, all in Sheila's distinctive colour palette.

In her latest collection, Free Spirit, Sheila has brought together an exuberant mix of silks and silk blend fabrics to capture the imagination and tempt you to reach out and touch. These are fabrics to add character, to excite the senses and provide individuality and charm. She gained her inspiration for the collection from a recent trip to the relatively unknown Himalayan Kingdom of Bhutan.

Whether your taste is for the comfortable and traditional or the contemporary and cutting edge, whether the project is contract or residential, Brian Yates is perfect for today's eclectic lifestyle.

Contact Details

Brian Yates
Lansil Way
Caton Road
Lancaster
LA1 3QY
Tel: 01524 35035
Fax: 01524 32232
Email: sales@brian-yates.co.uk
Website: www.brianyates.com

G27 Chelsea Harbour Design Centre
London
SW10 0XE
Tel: 020 7352 0123
Fax: 020 7352 6060

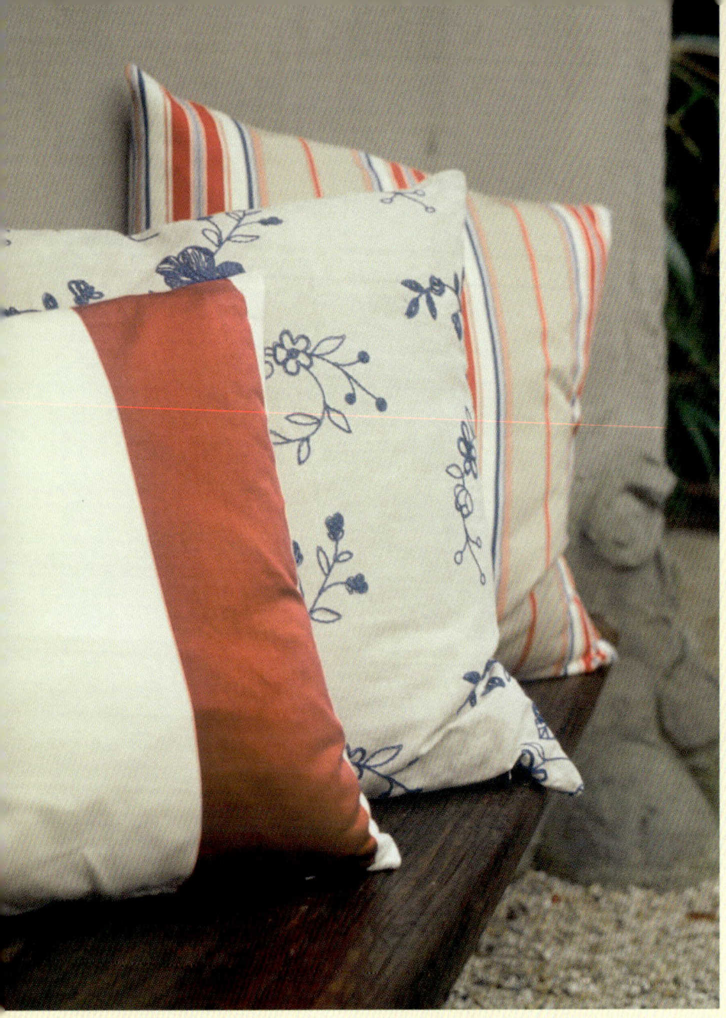

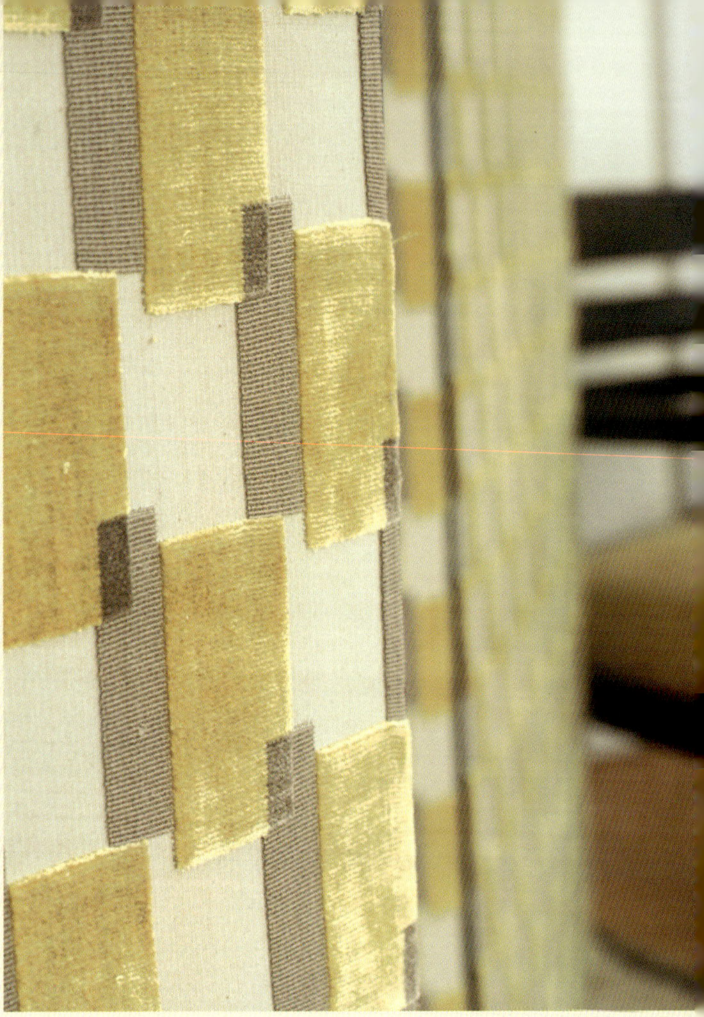

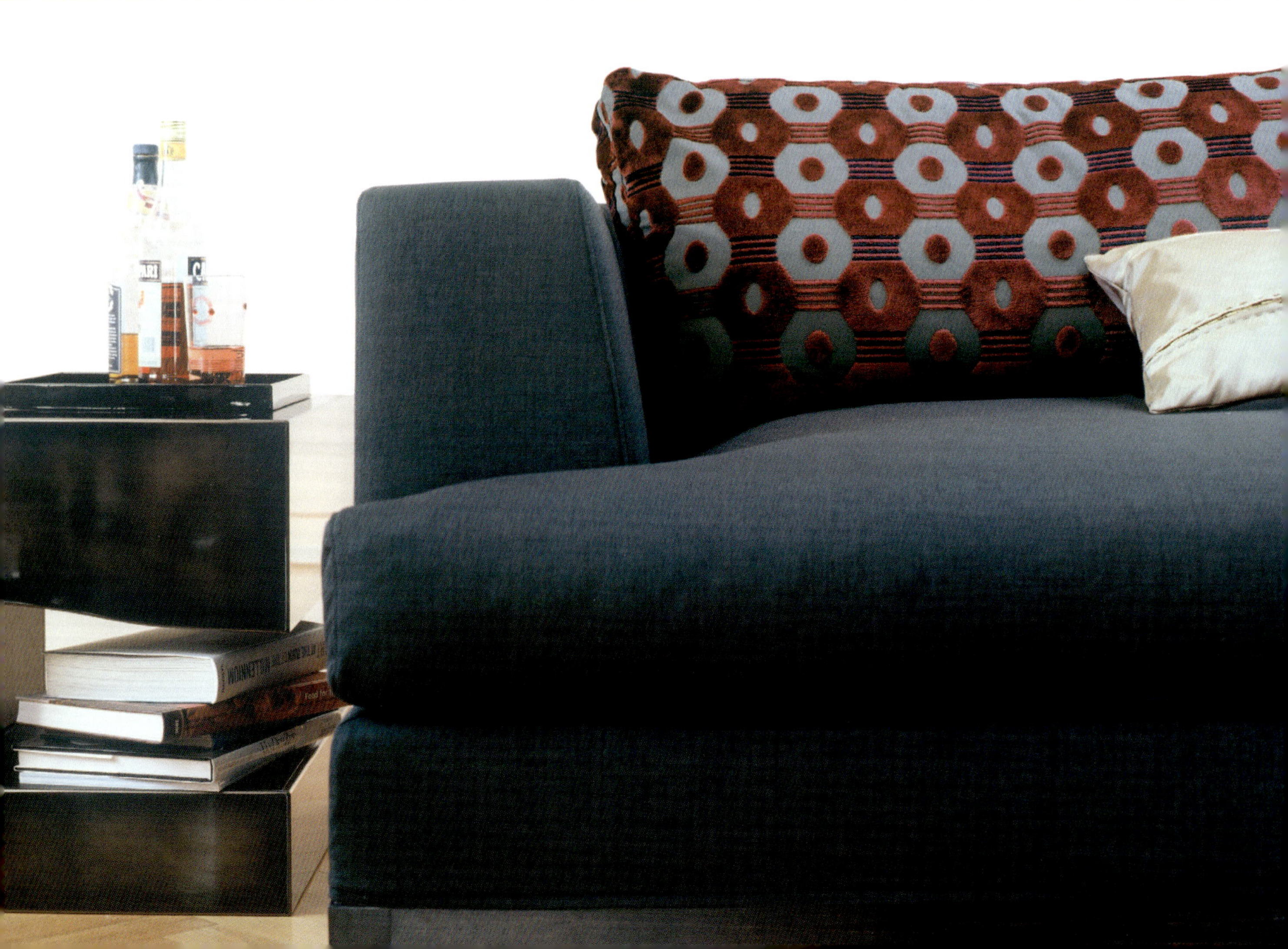

Zimmer+Rohde

A company renowned as much for its classic/contemporary style as its fresh, diverse fabrics, Zimmer + Rohde has the ability to cater to every taste.

Clockwise, from left: Sofa in the New Option fabric (1912-988) and back cushions covered in the Swing fabric (10060-386); Three cushions, fabrics used in (front to back): Dorran Stripe (10069-383), Dermott (10080-593), Dixon Stripe (10070-395); Fabric panel Charleston (10040-194); Silk stripe Revue (10061-415); Cushions in fabrics from the South Hampton collection; Curtain in Orfeo (4811-345) and chair in Daphne (2623-386), Ottoman in Impuls (1288-335); cushions on the bench in Revue and Mystery

Zimmer + Rohde specialises in plain textures in a huge diversity of colours, sumptuous silks, eclectic weaves and voiles. The three main collections typify the variety of styles it has to offer.

The Ardecora range was developed and designed in the company's Milan studio. It is classical in design, and has evolved an identity of its own. Opulence is its signature, and lustrous silks, damasks and velvets typify the range.

Etamine adds yet another dimension to the company. Fresh and lively in feel, Etamine is designed in the Paris studio.

Lastly, the Hodsell McKenzie collection, recently acquired by Zimmer + Rohde, brings a distinctive style of beautiful classic English prints and weaves.

From classic to cutting-edge contemporary, Zimmer + Rohde has something to inspire.

Contact Details

Zimmer + Rohde
14–15 Chelsea Harbour Design Centre
Lots Road
London
SW10 0XE
Tel: 020 7351 7115
Fax: 020 7351 5661
Email: info.uk@zimmer-rohde.com
Website: www.zimmer-rohde.com

Following the resounding success of the first collection launched in 2001, Zoffany has worked closely again with The National Trust to produce a sumptuous collection of weaves and wallpapers for Autumn/Winter 2005.

The collection consists of five weaves and seven wallpapers sourced from original National Trust references. Four historic properties, Ham House, Erddig House, Packwood House and Nostell Priory provide inspiration for both the collection of weaves, which includes richly textured damasks, velvets and appliqué silks, and also the lavish wallpapers which resemble iridescent silk, woodgrain and architectural trompes d'oeil.

WEAVES
Ham House Damask
Ham House (1610) on the Thames at Richmond contains a wealth of interior decoration and a distinguished collection of textiles. Among the furniture in the Queen's bedchamber is a set of fruitwood chairs upholstered in a silk velvet woven in Genoa, Spitalfields or Lyon around 1730. This fabric, now much degraded with its close-toned colours and velvet details, has been recreated as a silk and linen brocatelle. The main motif is interpreted in rich chenille woven over a subtle ombre warp. With a surrounding clover pattern, it sets off the lustre of the grounds.

Stuart Stripe
Between 1679 and 1683, the Queen's antechamber in Ham House was 'Hunge

Zoffany

This collection of weaves and wallpapers is as sensitive to British cultural heritage as it is forward thinking. It successfully connects the present with a rich cultural legacy.

The Percy Bass Decorator's Guide

with foure pieces of blewe Damusk (now faded to brown), impaned and bordered with blew velvet embroidered with gould and fringed'. Remarkably, these wallcoverings still exist in the Queen's antechamber as in this description. Stuart Stripe is composed from the design within the embroidered panels alternating with a contemporary Ottoman.

Spitalfields Velvet
Erddig House, near Wrexham in North Wales, was built by Joshua Edisbury in the late seventeenth century and completed after his death by John Meller in the eighteenth century. Much of the original furniture is still in the house today. The bold Spitalfields velvet on this furniture has inspired Spitalfields Velvet. Reconstructed in a quality that is suitable for both upholstery and drapes, the worn texture of the original fabric has been interpreted with a random dyed effect as a background to the trailing leaves and flowers.

Queen Mary's Silk
Packwood House in Warwickshire stands deep in Shakespeare's Forest of Arden and dates from that era. Queen Mary's Room in Packwood House was re-decorated for the Queen's visit in 1927. The room has a perfect late seventeenth-century panelled interior overlooking the yew garden with its stately topiary and beautifully kept lawns. The four-poster bed is hung with Italian green watered silk appliquéd with cream silk ribbons to make an unusual scrolling pattern with leaves. Elements of this elaborate border have been taken to create a subtle trellis design set with a simple leaf, and a coordinated design with a simple trellis. Woven in silk and linen, the design has an elegant simplicity that would suit both traditional and contemporary interiors.

WALLPAPERS
Nostell Priory
Nostell Priory is adapted from one of the India Papers, a hand-painted Chinese paper imported to the West by the East India Company and used in one of the bedrooms of Nostell Priory when they were re-decorated by Thomas Chippendale in the late eighteenth century. Nostell Priory depicts a flowering tree painted with the delicate detailing and tone work of the original wallpaper. It is available in six colourways, 69cm wide.

Ham House Damask
This design is inspired by an elaborate silk velvet dating from circa 1730, which covered a set of fruitwood chairs in the Queen's bedchamber at Ham House. The original fabric is now much degraded and this effect has been subtly recreated in the wallpaper texture. It is available in six colourways, 69cm wide.

Ham House Plain
The shot silk effect of this paper is taken from the background of Ham House Damask wallpaper to create an iridescent plain. Available in six colourways, 52cm wide.

Spitalfields
This design has been adapted from a Spitalfields velvet found at Erdigg House near Wrexham in North Wales. The effect of a cut and uncut epingle velvet has been rotary screen printed on a strie ackground. Available in seven colourways, 69cm wide.

Pennant Stripe
This wallpaper has been adapted from a wide and elaborate cornice in the Queen's bedchamber and the Queen's antechamber at Ham House. It has been drawn as a trompe l'oeil to give a three dimensional effect. Available in five colourways, 52cm wide.

Woodgrain and Woodgrain Border
The panelling of the Queen's antechamber in Ham House is painted with olivewood graining on a gilt ground. The bold scale and dark colouring over a subdued metallic gives an extraordinarily modern effect in this seventeenth-century house. The design has been interpreted as a wallpaper which would look equally fitting in a traditional or contemporary setting. The border can be used as a traditional wallpaper border or trimmed to create panels. Available in four colourways, paper 69cm wide, border 17.5cm wide.

Contact Details
Zoffany
Chalfont House
Oxford Road
Denham
UB9 4DX
Tel: 0870 830 0350
Fax: 0870 830 0352
Email: enquiries@zoffany.uk.com
Website: www.zoffany.com

Opposite, from top: Ham House damask in chocolate and Cranberry, £124 per metre; Spitalfield velvet in cerise, £95 per metre
Above, from top: Spitalfield velvet in green, £95 per metre; Queen Mary silk in gold, £100 per metre; Queen Mary silk in terracotta, £110 per metre

Jim Thompson, Crystal collection